THE WHISTLEBLOWER'S TUNE

A Memoir

HUGH GIBLIN

Black Rose Writing | Texas

ISBN: 978-1-68433-500-8
PUBLISHED BY BLACK ROSE WRITING
www.blackrosewriting.com

Printed in the United States of America
Suggested Retail Price (SRP) $18.95

The Whistleblower's Tune is printed in Sabon

*As a planet-friendly publisher, Black Rose Writing does its best to eliminate unnecessary waste to reduce paper usage and energy costs, while never compromising the reading experience. As a result, the final word count vs. page count may not meet common expectations.

To all the whistleblowers who have gone before me and those yet to come who have tried to do the right thing.

THE
WHISTLEBLOWER'S
TUNE

All Truths that are kept silent are poisonous.
- Nietzsche

CHAPTER ONE:
I GET STREET SENSE

My first exposure to the Mob took place when I was 11 years old. The Mob shot a man dead the previous night coming out of an Italian restaurant, a reputed Mob hangout in the neighborhood, about a block from our flat. I knew the "restaurant" which was on the first floor of a residential brownstone, however, it had always struck me as curious that I never saw customers going in or coming out of it.

The following day I went up to the corner and stared at the now black blood stain, which ran from the sidewalk near the curb and congealed on the street below it. Rain, feet and time would erase any traces of the crime, but I never erased the memory of it. I remember feeling uncomfortable with my voyeurism but I also remember it as an introduction to the violent nature of the "Outfit". I was also beginning to understand that "bad guys" did not always get caught the way the movies showed.

My neighborhood had a reputation from the 1920s when Al Capone killed seven men during the infamous St. Valentine's Massacre. This event happened at the SMC Cartage Company, at 2122 North Clark Street, a mile from our flat at 2838 Clark Street. I knew the warehouse building, torn down in 1965, perhaps to erase the notoriety of the building, but someone purchased the shot up wall which then wound up, ironically, in the men's room of a saloon. Finally, they broke it down into bricks and sold some, but most wound up in the Mob Museum in Las Vegas.

The Mob killed with impunity in Chicago, statistics say out of about 1400 Outfit killings from Capone's day police have solved fewer than 20. In the 1950s and 1960s, beatings and bodies in trunks were de rigueur for the Mob in Chicago; It was an essential part of their unique business model. For the hit-men there were no second chances, if they failed to kill their target the Outfit killed them. Two hit-men put three bullets in Ken Eto's head, he lived, they didn't.

The first time I blew the whistle in my life was when I was five years old and it was on my father. He was an Irish immigrant who worked as a switch-man for the Chicago Transit Authority and who drank heavily, (fortunately not on the job). He did it in painfully predictable cycles. On payday he would stop in at one of the neighborhood Irish bars, Dolan's or Timlin's, ostensibly for a few casual beers, and join a group of old country Irishmen who frequented the tavern. Then he would get into a card game, usually rummy, everybody would buy a round with each new deal and the shot and beers would keep coming. The afternoon turned into evening. Soon he was deep into the hard stuff, just whiskey; and later in the drinking cycle, the cheap stuff, wine. Then it was total alcohol immersion for days until his money and physical stamina ran out.

At the end of a drinking binge, sick with remorse and drying out, he'd go over to the parish church to "take the pledge" with the priest and solemnly vow to quit drinking. The priest would run him through the simple ritual, knowing full well, he'd see him again in a few months. My father would leave for his "fresh start" full of resolve and determination. Sadly, his resolve always faded in a few months, which he broke with the first drink. This was a self-destructive pattern of episodic alcoholism he followed for all of his adult life.

One event, one of my earliest memories, (around three years old) which borders on black comedy, happened when my father came home drunk and my mother refused to let him in our flat. He climbed up to the top of a large open transom above the door and tried to crawl into the flat, but got stuck up there like a stray cat up a tree. My mother called the police who pulled him down, took him away and held him overnight. I vividly remember this large Irish looking cop, who had put me and my brother on the dining room table while his partner got my father down, patting me on the head and looking at me with big sad eyes. He knew what was in my future.

Another time when I was five, I heard my father renounce drinking. So I was startled to see him, a few weeks later, with a half pint bottle of whiskey in his rear pants pocket. I was in the bedroom to take a nap, but was awake and watched as he hung up his pants on the door hook and got into bed. There was a strong odor of alcohol and tobacco on him. It seemed wrong to me because I had heard him promise my mother, after blowing his paycheck once more, that he would never do it again. I waited a few minutes then quietly got up and went out to the kitchen where my mother was cooking on the gas stove. "He's drinking again," I whispered. My father was right behind me in his underwear, "you little sneak" he yelled, "you damn little sneak". My mother reacted with protective anger. She waved the spatula, "leave him alone" she yelled, and he retreated. I stood there shaking.

Although he had shown no prior interest in me, his rejection of me from then on was clear, calculated and complete. I would stand at the front door waiting for him to come home after work and he would walk right past me without a word or a look. Those rare times he did family-like things, like fishing with my brother, he would not include me. Once, my father, who had never taken a moment's interest in my schooling, saw me doing my homework on the dining room table, "write you name," he said. It was a command not a request. I blocked. He went out into the kitchen and told my mother, "He doesn't even know how to write his name." To this day my signature is illegible. Perhaps I should have learned my lesson about the risks and rewards of whistleblowing from these unhappy early experiences but I didn't.

Then an experience I will never forget and that is still painful: I was on the back porch, the kitchen door open hoping for a lucky breeze in Chicago's torrid summer heat. We had on a big silver fan, which whirled ineffectively in the kitchen. My father was in the very unusual position of taking care of us kids, my mother having some compelling errand. I saw him in the kitchen and thought something was wrong between us and I should do something about it. So I went up to him and held up my arms. He sneered at me, "the sneaky one," he said, "what do you want?" He turned then and walked away. I felt something crush inside me and then a terrible void. I sat down heavily on a kitchen chair and stared at the floor. Years later, my sister for no apparent reason brought the day up. "He destroyed you that day," she said. She confirmed what I thought was something I may have imagined. Whenever I think of it, which isn't often, I still feel that moment, that same hurt. Time doesn't heal all wounds.

My response to the rejection afterwards was a strong defensive denial. I felt no anger or hurt instead it just seemed like I stopped feeling anything toward him. I knew my father had problems; I knew he was trying to hurt me; I viewed it just as an inescapable fact of my life. I was determined it would not bother me. I wrote him off as a father, expecting nothing and asking for nothing. I rigidly maintained this stance toward my father all his life, always maintaining a distinct distance, never yielding an inch. I knew he felt it. One time he looked at me and said, "Why do you always put the iron in it?" I didn't answer. Another time as a teen, I asked him for $10, more as a test than a need, to see if he might do it. Somewhat reluctantly, he gave it to me. That was the only time I asked my father for anything in my life (and I regret it, it spoiled an otherwise perfect record).

However, despite my best efforts to deny it, the rejection had a powerful impact on me. I withdrew into myself, stepped back somewhat from life, lost trust, and became hyper-vigilant. I was always watching people, listening to them, searching for something threatening in them. I expected the worst from people. I only felt comfortable when alone. Paradoxically, these unhealthy personality traits would prove helpful to me later in life.

When I was in fifth grade, sitting in the little wooden desks with round inkwells at St. Sebastian's Grammar School, the little Sisters of Charity nun was telling us about the fictional Don Quixote and his tilting with windmills while imagining them knights. The moral of the story was clear even to my young mind: unrealistic idealism is not rewarding. I also remember thinking *that's me, Don Quixote, that's what I'm like.* Now, in retrospect, I am impressed with the prescience of that eleven-year-old for that insight.

In seventh grade, I was the monitor who blew the whistle to the nun on Frankie, the class bully, for disrupting the return to the classroom after recess. The nun confronted Frankie with my report. Afterwards he threatened me, "never do that to me again,", he said. (I was tempted me to report that threat too but thought better of it). However, I had established my pattern, one that would reassert itself in dramatic fashion later in my life.

At twelve years old, I sold papers at a newsstand on the corner of Clark and Diversey, a half block from our flat. There were five corners at the busy intersection that had three major bus and streetcar lines and was an important transportation transfer point on the north-side. Within the immediate area was a retail section with dozens of storefront shops. The area west, north and south was working class with modest wood frame homes sheltering first or second generation German and Irish workers. Just east of the newsstand, down toward Lincoln Park and Lake Michigan, there were residential hotels, attractive apartment buildings, affluent brownstone residences and upscale restaurants. People who got off the bus and went east to their pricey homes were the professionals; ones that went west to their frame wooden houses or large old apartment buildings were the blue-collar workers. The geography of class.

I worked from 3 until 7 every weekday evening and from 9am until 7pm on Saturdays, 30 hours a week. Winters were brutal, mean. Wind whipping from Lake Michigan, two miles away, created a cruel wind chill factor that numbed the body and mind. The newsstand was made of painted black wood with some tin on the roof and was roughly six feet wide by four feet deep and eight feet high. The stand was open on one side so it provided scant shelter from the elements with about a foot of coverage for me. There were four stacks of papers of different publishers and editions on two fixed metal shelves in the stand with a dozen magazines displayed around the interior held up by wires strung across it.

We built a fire in a big steel drum and stamped our feet to avoid frostbite.

We cut the tops off our gloves so we could make the change. The cold would literally take my breath away and my fingers got so sore and rigid that I had to hold them in the flames to make them warm. In frigid snowstorms, I learned why animals stand in the wood, motionless like frozen statutes to keep their bodies warm and conserve energy. I was not always dressed well for the cold; I remember times when I had wet feet from holes in my shoes where the cardboard had rotted through and other times when I wasn't dressed adequately. I'll never understand how I escaped frostbite during those frigid winters. In fact, I rarely caught a cold or was sick.

Instead, I viewed it all as a challenge and took a perverse pride in being able to stand out in the weather, rejecting the option to go into the United Cigar store on the corner and watch the stand through the glass door. I was developing a stoicism that would serve me well in life. People complained to Jimmy, who owned the stand and, embarrassed, he used to order me to go into the cigar store. Jimmy, a grossly overweight, Italian immigrant with an omnipresent half-chewed cigar, and a checkered newspaper man's cap liked to gamble and often played cards at the streetcar barns evenings leaving me to watch the stand by myself. I was a conscientious worker, so Jimmy trusted me with the money. The only thing he didn't like about me was that I didn't "hustle" the papers but I was also a painfully shy boy and yelling out "paper" was both something I couldn't do nor wanted to do. He lamented the money he had lost during his life gambling. His sole advice to me was "save money kid even if it is only a dime a day."

Prior to my exposure to the street life of the corner, I led a sheltered life. Trying to escape from the hatred of my father and the empty poverty of my home life I had turned to what I felt was the safety and serenity of the church. As an altar boy from first grade through eighth grade, I spent an inordinate amount of time in church. I loved the rituals, the prayers, the hymns, the mystique of the mass. The ambiance of the church with its richly colored murals, stained glass, marble statutes, pure white linens, lighted white wax candles and ornate altar with shining gold-plated tabernacle had an irresistible, almost hypnotic lure for me. Each mass and benediction was magical to me. The murmured Latin prayers, the smell of incense, the solemn music, the dramatic movements of the priest in their colorful vestments were pure theater. This is where the bread and wine became consecrated and transformed into the body and blood of Christ and given to us in communion with Him.

I took my role as an actor in the drama seriously. I tried to make every prayer perfect and would repeat it over and over if my mind had wandered or if I felt the prayer was insincere. When I was lighting candles, I worried obsessively about knocking one over on the linen-covered altar. I struggled to learn the Latin prayers and faithfully served early masses, rising at 5:30 am and going to the church in all seasons. I liked walking the half mile to the church; the streets were quiet, little traffic, or people, it was like a little pilgrimage each time. I often substituted for other altar boys who were no shows. The rituals and my religious training had a powerful moral influence on me. People began talking about me becoming a priest. I would disappoint them.

The darker side of this absorption in religion was that I was institutionalizing my sense of unworthiness. My father's rejection, despite my conscious efforts to brush it aside as irrelevant, left me feeling unacceptable, unworthy, and unlovable. (If your own father wouldn't love you who could?). I was certain that there was something wrong with me, something not good enough. The Catholic Church's focus on sin (including the Original one from birth, a dark moral defect imprinted on one's soul to start life with) contributed to that sense of unworthiness. Striving for moral perfection fitted my strong need to make myself good, worthy, and acceptable. Sin was omnipresent in Catholicism. One mortal sin against the Seventh Commandment, (mostly about sex), not confessed, and unforgiven could send you to Hell for eternity. The Holy Family: Mary, Joseph, and Jesus became my family. I was told they loved me and I would never have to worry about rejection from them.....as long as I was good.

Being good was the most important thing in my life. Our fifth grade nun, a woman with an earned reputation as *mean*, used to go on disciplinary tantrums. One day she went around the room, methodically hitting the back of everyone's hand once with a ruler; when she came to me she put the ruler down and walked to her desk,(I thought for a giddy moment that she had overlooked me or she considered me too virtuous to hit). But she picked up a thick geography book and hit me flat on the head with it. "And you," she said, "you're too good." Some other kids clapped, and I knew they agreed with her. I was a *goody-two-shoes*. It hurt my feelings much more than my head, "too good" I said to myself, "How can anyone be *too* good."

Outside the church, I was a quiet, introspective kid. I had no close friends and went my own way. My classmates accepted me "as is" and I accepted them the same way, and we lived in a kind of compatible co-existence. No one bothered or bullied me, although I would have made an easy target. Despite my early whistleblowing experiences, I was not a tattle-tale and strictly minded my own business unless something involved me directly. My quietness gave me a protective cloak, people forgot I was around and I was rarely a center of attention and never a point of contention. I was developing a "style", a way of coping with the world, a way of working on the margins of life neither getting all the way in or all the way out. This low profile mode of functioning would be invaluable in my future whistleblowing.

I was afraid of people. People called me shy, but it went deeper than that. I hated myself for that timidness, but the fear seemed deeply ingrained. I had gone into a protective shell after my experience with my father and I wasn't able to break out. I was very watchful, always scrutinizing, even when I was participating. Adults found me polite but my emotional distance would make them uncomfortable, especially if they alone with me. My relatives would say to my mother, "He's a deep one" or "He always seems to be thinking." My mother worried about my "social backwardness" with my Uncle Johnny, "Don't worry about it," he said, brushing it off. "He'll grow out of that." I didn't.

The corner was a culture shock for me. I saw hundreds of different people every day. I got to know the faces and styles of those who bought papers. Most were always in a hurry, especially in bad weather, the purchase of a newspaper their most incidental transaction of the day and an impersonal one. I learned to make change quickly and accurately with one hand, the other snapping the newspaper from under the iron bar on top of the bundle that kept them from blowing away, folding it and giving it to the customer all in one quick motion. The only perk I had was the ability to take comic books home to read and return them the next day, the days of Superman, Batman, Dick Tracy, Joe Palooka, Dagwood, Little Orphan Annie, etc. I read the papers every day, especially but not exclusively, the sports section (as a Cub fan I learned early the virtue of accepting losing with patience). I also started to learn about Chicago politics and the Outfit.

There were incidents on the corner. Sometimes older kids would try to hit me up for money, which I refused. One time Lester, one of the local young "Diversey Gang" who hung out on another corner, asked for money. When I refused he tried to grab some money out of my change apron and when I resisted attempted to knee me in the groin sending coins from my change bag flying over the corner. He ran off with no money and I, shaken but unhurt, dutifully picked up the coins. Months later, when I was walking by his house on Orchard Street he came out toward me. I braced myself for the worst but what he wanted to do was apologize. He was a blond kid with a grown up face, "How you doing," he said. I muttered an "okay". "Sorry about what happened," he said and ran back across the street. I liked his apology. Later I found out they arrested him for auto theft and sent to a correction center for kids.

The Diversey gang jived around on the opposite corner, talking loud, laughing, pitching pennies, making sure passer-byes felt their presence. The cops left them along as long as there weren't fights. I got to know the names of some: Dago, a cross-eyed tough kid, Snooky, a small, sneaky looking kid with a cap and suede shoes, Ace, a self-bestowed name, something of an athlete. Larry, a small guy who got by on his wit and gang savvy, and Jerry Schmidt, a big, muscular older guy who was the heavy of the gang. They did crazy things sometime. One went down to the Lincoln park Zoo and shot up a bunch of rare birds. Jerry Schmidt has this peace treaty with Louie the Mex from another gang. The guys were always debating who was the toughest hoping for a showdown, never happened, nobody in the gang messed with Jerry. Some years later they arrested him with some others in a stupid strong -arm robbery of a guy with a briefcase who they thought had money in it. I'm sure he did time for that one.

And there were instances of kindness on the corner. The Greek manager of the Hollywood Barbecue restaurant occasionally would ask me to bring him a paper of a certain edition at a specific time. When I brought it over, he would give me a barbecue dinner with french fries all wrapped up to go as a tip (he could have easily walked across the street to get the paper at any time). Other times I would get an extra nickel or dime tip when I sold a paper. The guys in the cigar store were always welcoming when I came in from the cold. Some people would bring back a clean paper after they read it so I could resell it for myself. Fats, a guy who worked as a printer at the Chicago Tribune, would bring me a bunch of papers that I could sell for my own benefit. I've never forgotten those compassionate, human touches.

We struggled to survive at home. My father's drinking made life financially precarious. paydays were often pay-less for us It all came down one day when my father hit my mother during a quarrel. He had drank and gambled away another paycheck. When I came home from school, I saw a broken bottle on the floor, the table in disarray and food left unfinished in pots on the stove. And no mother. I knew something bad had happened. I saw her later coming down the street with a sad smile and a black eye. She patted me on the head but said nothing. That pat on the head was a foreboding of things to come. She got him out of the house under a peace bond and he never got back in.

I was twelve. "Buddy, (my nickname), will have to go to work," she said, and she got me the job at the newsstand. Often toward the end of a week, we ran out of money for food and carfare. My mother would be at the kitchen table saying, "I don't know what we are going to do next week. I don't have a dollar left." I would go to a drawer in the living room where I kept my little cache of tips and earnings and lay it on the kitchen table in front of my mother. Her look of sad gratitude always touched me.

Nobody calls me "Buddy" anymore, at times, I forget I ever had the name. It came from the time I was a baby without a name. My mother contracted what they called in those days, "double pneumonia" during my birth, came close to death and in the hospital for six months. So they separated us from birth, the concern was that I would be vulnerable to the disease.

I was first placed in the nursery where I, in time, became the biggest baby there and an object of some attention by visitors who thought I was a newborn. The hospital had to discharge me because of the bill, and they placed me in the care of relatives who passed me from one to another over six months. This separation according to some therapists may have accounted for my emotional detachment later in life, the theory being I hadn't bonded properly. Maybe. But I didn't know her and didn't have any sense of time and the relatives who took care of me might have seemed like mothers to me. Then again, one spends nine months knowing the body, the smells, the taste of the mother and might sense that loss if separated. I don't know the real answer to this experience.

There were other guys who hung around the corner. Lefty, a huge man with a prominent broken nose and an impassive face always wore a black topcoat and a gray cap and was a fixture on the corner. He stood there stoically in all kinds of weather, hardly moving in front of the cigar store, his eyes scanning the street and smoked a seemingly never finished cigar. (He reminded me of the classic wooden Indian in front of an old time cigar stores). Although Lefty and I shared the corner for two years, he never said a word to me, in fact, he never seemed to notice me. He would stand there at specific times every day, still, like a towering statue, taking "off track" bets on the horse races which in those days was illegal. The horse-players would come to Lefty, say hello and shake his hand, slipping him the bet.

Lefty would deftly slide the bet into his huge topcoat pocket and the transaction was over. This little sleight of hand ritual, while obvious in its intent, had to be discreet to avoid offending the non-betting public and the police by being too blatant. Little George, the neighborhood bookie, would come by later to pick up the bets and cash stacked in Lefty's pocket and go off to either place the bets or cover some himself. Little George was a small, mean looking man, with a hard, pinched face and weak blue eyes, who dressed in a camel's hair coat, matching fedora, loud tie, and expensive jewelry. They told me he once was a bellboy at a neighborhood hotel. He never talked to me either.

We had local characters who often came around the corner or passed through it: "Father Time" a smiling, rotund man dressed casually in a sports coat and hat came with a large windup, ticking alarm clock around his neck which covered part of his chest. He walked around, a mobile life-sized human replica of an antique grandfather clock. I always had the feeling he was putting everybody on and enjoying himself immensely. I remember always checking his clock to see if it was the right time. It never was, but that detail didn't seem to bother Father Time one bit; a good time, not the right time, was his goal.

And the "chicken man" a gray-haired skinny black man with a wild kinetic energy, who carried a live chicken with him everywhere he went, even on the streetcar, all the while carrying on an incessant chatter with the chicken. The passengers and bus drivers viewed him as bizarre but welcomed a bit of diversion and entertainment from the boredom of just another bus trip. One time I saw him yelling and running up Clark Street chasing after his chicken. He became something of an urban legend and I've read about him in stories set in Chicago. (His photo is on the Internet).

And old Bill, a large, gentle looking man with a dignified demeanor, who always wore a shabby three piece suit with tie and a gray deformed hat. While lucid at one moment, he would stop in the middle of the street and briefly engage in an animated argument with the pope, solemnly waving his finger to point out problems with Roman Catholicism. Motorists, surprisingly patient, waited until he finished. He was friendly in a somewhat formal, grandiose way and always bowed and said hello to familiar faces on the street, tipping his hat to women.. The folk rumor in the neighborhood was that he was an attorney who lost everything during the Great Depression, including his mind. Almost everybody in the neighborhood had a biography, mostly folk tales, with a grain of truth, elaborately embellished.

There was Rocco, a young Italian punk who would stand on the corner flipping a coin, just to be seen. He was a wannabe wiseguy. He always gave up the corner when Lefty came around to do business. "Smiley" a boy with very prominent buck teeth worked on another stand owned by Jimmy, which was diagonal from mine in front of Andes Candies. He was a nice, hardworking kid from a poor family. His mother and sister, dressed with the same formless, colorless clothes and stringy hair were a study in poignant poverty as they brought Smiley his lunch on Saturday. I remember his face, red from the cold with his nose running, wearing a stocking head cover which, coupled with his perpetual smile, gave him a dunce like appearance. I wonder what happened to Smiley in life.

Up Clark Street was the barbershop bookie where my father placed his racetrack bets and often left a large part of his paycheck. The Irish seemed to have a soft spot for horses either riding them or betting on them or both. Dan Milano, the owner of the reputed restaurant/Mob hangout who was also the precinct captain, used to come around the corner once in a while. He was a small, soft-spoken, grandfatherly man who always used to smile and say "hello kid" as he passed by the stand. The police bothered nobody on the corner although they had to know what was going on there. Police on the take were another Chicago phenomenon.

As a kid I learned the Outfit, then called the "Syndicate" had their hands in a lot of things: juke boxes, restroom supplies, racetrack wire services, bookmaking, pornography, crap games, juice loans, bars, unions, insurance companies, restaurants even banks. A Senate committee headed by Estes Kefauver, a Senator from Tennessee, had held hearings on the

Chicago Mob back in the Fifties and there was a lot of publicity, but nothing came of them. Years later, New York Times reporters wrote how the Outfit had blackmailed Kefauver. They set him up and photographed him in a sexual escapade in the Drake hotel, which led him to compromise his organized crime investigation in Chicago.

People talked about the Outfit with awed respect for their naked power and influence. The mayor and the police accepted them as a fact of life. I had a simple but a strong sense of right and wrong and it bothered me that hoodlums could bully society with their crude and brutal methods and it disturbed me that nobody seemed to be able to do much about it. I didn't like the fact that people merely accepted it as another fact of Chicago life just like the weather.

So long before the "Godfather" and the "Sopranos" I knew something about the Mob. The Mob is part of the folklore for Chicagoans, who, like Westerners and their cowboy gunfighters, take a perverse pride in their outlaws and Mobsters. They were good copy for the Chicago newspapers with frequent gory hits and decaying bodies turning up in the trunks of cars. They had colorful nicknames the papers loved to put in parentheses: Anthony (Joe Batters) Arcardo, later the head of the Chicago "Outfit, Joey (Doves) Auippa, Murray (the Camel) Humphreys, Paul, (the Waiter), Ricca, Sam, (MoMo) Giancana, Jake (the Barber) Factor, Joey, (the Clown) Lombardo, et al. The Italians, having disposed of the Irish Mob with the killing of Dion O'Bannion in the Thirties, dominated the organized crime scene in Chicago thereafter. Never in my deepest, darkest fantasies did I ever think I would have any kind of relationship with these people.

CHAPTER TWO:
I GET A NEW JOB

Chances rule men, and not men chances.
- Aratabanus (Ancient King of Persia)

The labyrinthine connections of life could almost make one believe in fate. I'm always intrigued by how the past interweaves itself into the future. Over three decades later, in 1985, I interviewed for a job with an international labor union in Washington, D.C. Living in North Carolina working through the end of a three-year relationship with a woman, I was doing some hard soul-searching, not just on the end of the relationship, but on what I had accomplished (or more candidly had not accomplished) during my accounting career. I felt some deep dissatisfaction with the answers I came up with in that retrospective effort.

I spent 20 years working in government, corporations, public accounting and the last six of those years in nonprofit groups. While making some serious efforts toward what I considered was something of a contribution to society by working as a consultant in the nonprofit world. I couldn't point to anything that I had accomplished that felt all that satisfying or meaningful. I felt more like a dilettante who was dabbling in contributing rather than making one. This feeling haunted me, I had this need to do something important, something that would really count something that would make a difference. The people I admired most were the ones who gave it their all, their life's efforts and sometimes their lives to make that difference. That wasn't me.

I checked the Sunday Washington Post every week and found a blind ad placed by a CPA firm for an unnamed union that was screening applicants for an accounting position. I thought I would find more meaning working full time in the labor movement, becoming part of an organization rather than just consulting with it. I found out from the response to the ad that the union was the Hotel Employees and Restaurant Employees International Union (HEREIU). Their letter was casual, informal for a CPA firm. "Stop in and see us if you come up to D.C." it said. I called and set up an interview. I had spent most of the summer in Chapel Hill, North Carolina, waiting for my lady friend to get a job and settle in. She did that and I was free to go. I packed, parted congenially from her and started the trip up to D.C. in the motor home. On the drive up I worried. I knew of the union's volatile and violent past in Chicago and I wondered whether there were Mob problems at the international union level.

Once in D.C., a half hour before the interview, I stopped at an "M" street payphone and called Heather Booth, a legendary Chicago activist and founder of the activist training organization, the Midwest Academy. I knew she had a broad knowledge of the union world. I told her I worried about possible organized crime influence in the union and asked, "Are there any problems in the International?" She was positive about the union saying that it had taken some progressive steps in recent years. "Well, you know they've had problems here" she said, "I don't know about any in the International, I know they've been doing some good things in organizing, some pretty progressive stuff." "I got a call for a reference" she continued, "told them you worked like a dog." I thanked her and hung up. Feeling better about the upcoming interview. I figured that any organized crime influence was in the big city locals, not the International union. I was wrong.

I was screened in the office of Thomas Havey & Company, a CPA firm which had over 700 union clients, the most of any accounting firm in the country, including several teamster and laborer locals. Havey had five offices nationally including the one in D.C. where I interviewed. Frank Massey, the union's managing accounting partner, a man who looked like the late actor Peter Sellers, replete with a mustache, seemed amused when I told him I wanted to contribute and work in the labor movement. He asked no questions but sat behind his desk, leaned back in his chair and looked over my resume.

When he noticed I had worked in Chicago, he warmed up "You're from Chicago". I only nodded, one thing I had learned in many interviews was to let the interviewer do more talking than I did. "I go to Chicago a lot", he said smiling," We're headquartered right there on La Salle Street, you know, yeah Chicago is a great town." I nodded again. Later I realized this recognition on his part may have gotten me the job since several officers were from Chicago and he may have thought I was being quietly referred to him by one of them. The interview ended quickly, and he sent me over to see the International's Secretary-Treasurer.

The interviews at the union were just as perfunctory: I met with the Secretary-Treasurer, Herman (Blackie) Leavitt, a small, slight man in his seventies, who despite the graying of age, still had some of dark physical ambiance that gave him his nickname. He was well-dressed, almost dapper. He made some small talk, seemed somewhat distracted and asked none of the usual questions one expects during an interview. He barely looked at my resume, just held it in his hand on the desk, "You know about accounting?" "Yes" I said. "You think you can handle this job for us'?" I did not understand what specific job he was talking about and figured he must be just testing my confidence, 'Yes" I said. Following some moments of uncomfortable silence I felt I should say something to fill in the conversation hiatus and I asked him how he felt after a long career in labor. "I don't know" he said and shrugged, "I don't know" he repeated. He acted as if I had asked him a question he had never considered before. I began to have a sense that this job would be different.

He turned the interview over to his aide, a slight blond man in his forties who avoided eye contact and was an ineffective interviewer. He impressed me then, and always afterwards, as someone who was acting his role rather than living it, like a bad actor in a play whose lines don't ring true. He told me my job would be to help develop and implement an accounting program that would do the "check-off". "We want to put it and computers into all the local unions", he said.

The check-off is a list of union members whose records are checked off as the member pays their dues or through withholding by the employer. It is the traditional way of collecting union dues from members, the "bread and butter" of labor unions. The International wanted to put all its locals on a computer to make, not only their dues collection more efficient, but the payment of the "per capita" tax, (that portion of the dues of each member that goes to the International union), more effective. I waited in the next room while Leavitt and his aide consulted about me. The door was open, "I don't know about this guy," I heard Leavitt saying. "Frank wouldn't steer us wrong," the aide said. Leavitt said nothing. I had the feeling they hired me. Much later Leavitt expressed regret about my hiring saying aloud one time when talking about it, "why don't I listen to my instincts?"

The Hotel Employees and Restaurant Employees International Union began its turbulent life in 1866 in Chicago known then as the Bartenders and Waiters Union. The fledgling union joined the Knights of Labor in 1880 and when that organization ended, the union joined the American Federation of Labor in 1891. Chicago in the late nineteenth century was a ferment of union activity. The Bartenders and Waiters union which started with a few members, all male and mostly immigrants with some Socialists, had at its peak, in the 1970s, 488,000 members. Threatened during its long history by both Communists and racketeers, the union, at least at the International level, dealt with these unwanted influences with considerable success fighting off powerful Mob efforts to take over the union in the Thirties and Communist influence in the Fifties.

From what I've read the men who led the union in the years prior to the Seventies appear to be dedicated union leaders with the ability and perseverance to survive the long hard struggle for unionization of the culinary workers. Worker such as bartenders, waiters and waitresses, chefs, maids, bellhops, desk clerks, hostesses, casino workers, nurses' aids, all those ubiquitous souls who are at our beck and call to make our lives more comfortable and convenient. These are service jobs people like to call "unskilled" but it's been my experience that there are few jobs that don't require skills in servicing the very diverse and sometimes demanding public. One sociological study found that waitresses suffer more stress than business executives.

The International had 175 local unions in all the states including Alaska and Hawaii and Canada and Puerto Rico (hence the name "International"). In some areas in the South, the union's presence was insignificant. However, in places like Las Vegas, Atlantic City and Hawaii, where the hospitality industry is dominant, the union was a powerful player in politics and the local economy with tens of thousands of members. There are few active diners or frequent hotel guests in our major cities who have not bumped into a hotel or restaurant strike by HEREIU workers at some time in their lives. I remember being in San Francisco with my lady friend and finding a picket line walking the sidewalk in front of the restaurant we were going to. We talked with them a bit and walked off. The strikers thanked us profusely.

The International's headquarters was in a converted three-story former school building in historic and fashionable Georgetown in D.C., close to a townhouse where president Kennedy had lived as a young Congressman. The union's president, Edward T. Hanley, had moved the union's headquarters from Cincinnati to D.C. in 1984. Ed Hanley, a boyhood friend of the former powerful Illinois Congressman Ed Rostenkowski, and an ardent admirer of the original Mayor Richard Daley, wanted to bring Chicago style politics to D.C., i.e., money transformed into political clout. He did it well.

Ed Hanley

Hanley was a big man with Irish good looks to compliment his strong personal physical presence. He had a good sense of humor and considerable charm all of which he used to good effect. One local president told me he had gotten upset with Hanley during a convention speech and yelled out "who does he think he is God?" Later, in the bar, Hanley came over to him smiling and said, "I forgive you my son." He had won over the local president. Another officer had a darker take on Hanley, telling me about a time when he arrived at the union local drunk with an "assistant "who was packing a gun and showing it off.

Hanley grew up in Chicago, the son of James "Stick" Hanley, who owned and ran a tavern. Ed Hanley's sister married into the Mob via a man named Frank Calabrese., boss of the Outfit's 26th Street Mafia crew. Hanley graduated from high school in 1949 and dropped out of both Loyola University and Wright Junior College, completing no courses. He enlisted in the Air Force and spent two years in service in the Fifties.

After discharge he worked for finance companies, (and was said to have helped Mafia leaders, Accardo and Aiuppa, with their gambling loans by pulling their files at critical collection times, a favor for which they fired him). Afterwards went to work as a bartender in his father's tavern and became a member of local 450. Later he became a business agent for the Mob run local and began his startling rise in the ranks of organized labor becoming president of the local union in 1964. He became president of the International in 1973 at age 41; he married that same year.

Accardo

The International Union had spared no expense in converting the old red brick school building and it had an almost museum quality to it. Security was tight. A lock-less motion sensor system was in place on the doors and windows, the rear doors to the garage had thick steel plating (like the ones in Twenties speakeasy films). There was a former Virginia cop, the security man, who walked around unconsciously patting his shoulder holster all the time. The employees had that independent spirit one finds in union members, and they followed starting and quitting times religiously. A new IBM computer was in place and the union was modernizing its procedures which were seriously antiquated, more like an early 20th century style workplace, labor intensive, paper inundated and cumbersome.

I had a cubicle in the basement near the bookkeeping department. I was spending my time helping set up a payroll on the computer and learning about the union. I had a feeling I was into something but I wasn't sure exactly what. When I saw Jackie Pressor, later notorious head of the Teamsters and a well known Chicago Mob figure, John Lardino's names on a previous payroll I became very curious. It was like reading the promising first paragraph of a novel, sure there was more interesting material to come. I wanted to read more chapters.

About a month after I started, I picked up a financial statement an auditor had left on a desk and looked it over. Accountants read financial statements like some people read menus. The union had about 16 million in assets and had revenues of around 30 million dollars yearly from per capita dues, numbers equivalent to a small business corporation. What startled me was almost one and a half million in loans receivable carried on the books from two large loans that went bad; and there was a 2.5 million dollar Sabre jet; a hundred thousand dollar motor home, a D.C. luxury condo plus a very large payroll expense with officer's salaries leading the way absorbing over 10% of revenues alone.

These figures didn't include expense accounts, pensions, and other perks for officers. I remembered reading where the Teamsters had used bad loans to groups who went mysteriously bankrupt as a technique of siphoning off large amounts of cash illegally.

Suddenly, I had an intense curiosity to check this out. The numbers triggered, not only a curiosity, but a kind of excited tension in me. I had a feeling there was a lot more to learn about the union's finances. The following evening, after five, I was in the accounting department going through the files looking for details on the loans. After a few minutes sorting thru the files, I had that uncanny feeling that someone was watching me. The room was dark, the overhead lights off and only the light filtering in from the street gave the room some visibility. I angled my body over slightly as to get a better view of the room and I saw a blonde woman in a darkened cubicle standing motionless watching me. I closed up the file drawer and left. The next day, as a cover, talking to the head bookkeeper I mentioned, as casually as I could, that I had been looking for a file the night before in his department. The story worked with him but not the blonde woman who saw in my demeanor at the files the truth.

She told her boyfriend from Chicago, a barrel chested, powerfully built man named Barney Grogan, who had the title of research director. I later learned he had served two terms, totaling fifteen years in Alcatraz, one for robbing a bank and the other for securities fraud. He was in Alcatraz the same time as the notorious Whitey Bulger and they became close friends. In fact, Grogan is reputed to have helped Bulger when he was on the run in 1994. Grogan had the nickname "Dirty Shirt" from stealing steaks from the Alcatraz kitchen and hiding them under his shirt. He died in 2004 of natural causes a few days before the FBI would question him on Bulger's whereabouts.

Barney Grogan

He was a gregarious man who came into the office in the morning singing or talking and seemed to have a powerful need for attention., (in contrast to his nickname or maybe because of it he dressed nattily). Grogan was one of those talkative Irish-American types I knew too well who would continue talking to you knowing you were desperate to end the conversation and get on with your day, (I believe if I were talking to one of them on the phone in a burning building with the roof ready to collapse and told them I had to leave or die they would just keep right on talking). We talked a lot about Chicago, the neighborhoods, the politics. He knew the city well. He knew all the guys on the corner: Lefty, Little George, and Dan Milano. "Milano", he said, "he's still alive, you know."

Grogan, an Irish-American Catholic, had grown up in St. Patrick's parish on Chicago's west side where here he played football and said to have returned a punt for 103 yards for a touchdown, a school record at the time. He fancied himself an intellectual of sorts; he was interested in history and could, in fact, come up with some interesting historical facts. It was clear he had done a lot of reading during his time on the "Rock" but an intellectual he was not. He talked freely about doing time. "I've done some stupid things in my life Hughie," he would say, less with regret than resignation. "I survived," he said to me one time about his time in Alcatraz, "I survived Hughie."

We would test each other on the geographic knowledge of city streets and north-side neighborhoods trying to one up each other with details of the streets. I would try to think of some short little used street near a museum and that stumped him. He was better on the little-known west side streets where he grew up. I enjoyed our bantering, but I sensed he was always measuring me beneath the superficial chatter. He knew I wasn't one of them. (Although when he first met me he thought I was "on the run") A short time after the incident in the accounting files, he told a group of us an anecdote about an informer who had been tossed out of a window from an upper story hotel room in Chicago. He laughed heartily as he told it but I read it as a message for me and I suspended my explorations into the files.

I was suspect among a small group of people. The blonde woman continued her surveillance of me, sometimes standing outside the window on the street watching me after hours. One day I was on the phone talking to an acquaintance from Chicago, a librarian who worked at the Library of Congress. We were arranging a tennis game when suddenly during the conversation there were rasping noises on the phone. My friend cried out, "Your phone is being tapped". I laughed it off and said it was his supervisor checking up on him for goofing off, but I was tight inside and knew he could be right. A week passed, and I was suspecting myself of paranoia when coincidentally I overheard the office manager complaining to a co-worker about the wiretapping going on in the union. My friend had been right after all! My guess is that it was Grogan, and he screwed up the bug.

Around this time, the staff received a bushel of Washington apples, an annual gift from the president of the Seattle local, Mario Vacarino. A week later, we learned he was beaten and then drowned in his home's bathtub. There was some speculation the killing was over his resistance to his local joining the International's welfare funds but, much later, further investigation implicated a professional killer hired by a disgruntled union employee. The bookkeeper who had by then heard about my file caper pointedly told me about the murder, the subtext being "you better be careful". I was.

I stopped working late and made no more solo forays into the files. I decided I had blundered badly on my first attempt at exploring and that I had better cool it for a while. I was going to walk a very straight line. They cleaned the rugs at the International that week, prompting a comment by the accounting partner. "What, they're cleaning the rugs again; they just did that two weeks ago!" The aide shrugged and gave no reply. But I knew why they were cleaning the rugs; they were looking for bugs. I had raised their suspicions.

The International didn't like people who asked too many questions. They pulled a young auditor from the Havey firm off the audit for asking "too many questions". I also remember a young African-American woman in accounts payable who got transferred to another job because she wanted documentary support for expenditures. The message to the staff was clear: do what you're told, don't ask why you're doing it, don't look for trouble. The experienced personnel took that message to heart. They had a comfortable, secure, well-paying job with excellent benefits and they weren't looking to jeopardize those job perks by asking too many questions irrespective of whether expenses were legitimate. They didn't consider that part of their job description. That business was none of theirs. We all know how to compartmentalize things mentally, a sort of like packing luggage for a trip separating incongruous things.

The technical development of the program was in the hands of a programmer working for the Thomas Havey firm in Chicago. My function was to provide him with guidance on the accounting aspects of the program. He was a Phd, a former academic who trained himself in programming. I found him a congenial and an interesting partner in the project. I knew accounting but little programming, and he knew programming but little accounting. We complemented each other well with our mutual ignorance and knowledge. I had a lot to learn about computer hardware and software, but I'm a learner and I immersed myself into the subject. I read as many manuals, magazines, and books that I could find. Soon I was talking the jazzy jargon of computer jargon: RAM, bytes, megahertz, DOS, networks, software, floppy disks, etc. But I knew I would never make a good technical person, my mind was wired to liberal arts, the humanities not tech.

The programmer and I spent a lot of time on the phone discussing the program and it began to take shape for installation into the locals. I learned that developing a program was far from the scientific process I had imagined it to be and was a grueling project of trial and error, testing and retesting requiring patience and determination. It was as much a test of the character of the developers as a test of the program itself. The programmer had no idea of any organized crime problems in the union; He was an ivory tower type whose academic background provided him with a lot of learning but little street sense.

The program was Herman Leavitt's pet project, and he wanted it done by the next convention so he could claim the credit for modernizing the union. Leavitt, rumor had it, was an orphan born in Chicago, had spent his labor career in organizing. He seemed to have little business experience, despite the positions he had held, leaving most of the details to his aide who had almost as little sophistication. Although it might have been age related too, one time he stood in his office holding his head, "my fucking memory" he said, trying to remember what he was going to do next. I was startled, then amused, one day while Leavitt and his aide tried to figure out how much simple interest one would receive on a hypothetical million dollars at ten percent in a year, a computation the average high school student could accomplish without a calculator. They turned to me for the answer. I paused, trying to treat the question with the respect it didn't deserve and gave them the number.

There was, in reality, with very few exceptions, little in the way of business sophistication at the International although it may be more accurate to say it was as much lack of concern and lack of business acumen. Many of the officers were men who started as waiters, bellhops, bartenders and then moved up the ranks, the general vice-president had been a bellhop at one time. I wouldn't have expected them to manage like Harvard MBAs but the problem was that money didn't seem to be an issue in their decisions. Bills and expense accounts, including personal expenses, paid without documentation or concern for their authenticity or reasonableness; raises were extraordinarily large for some, (I saw one employee double his salary from 35k to 70k in less than six months and a well-paid-secretary receive an ad hoc spontaneous increase of $15,000 per year).

All the officers and some staff had leased cars along with paid automobile insurance, some just to commute to work, and per diem payments for travel, although not all traveled. Payroll, expenses, and benefits alone were almost fifty percent of the revenues of the International, (a percentage that might be more appropriate for an NBA team). I was in the office with Leavitt one afternoon and we were talking about some jobs in the union, Leavitt, always the realist, said, "You would have to be crazy to quit a job like this."

My job title at the union was an administrative aide, although I was in essence an accountant. I majored in accounting and business in the Evenings Division at Northwestern University in Chicago after discharge from the Army. After dropping my first course in night school I went to the Veteran's Administration and took a three-day series of aptitude tests along with psychological tests culminating in an interview with a psychologist. They told me I scored high in an aptitude for accounting and literature. I remember thinking *literature, what good is having an aptitude in literature?* I felt I needed to survive, earn a living, and learn a trade. Survival not fulfillment was my motivation. I opted for a degree in business administration and began taking accounting and business courses. Unfortunately, I miscast myself. Accounting was never a labor of love for me but simply a job.

With two courses behind me, I went looking for accounting jobs. I was an accounting clerk in corporate accounting departments for a few years while I learned the trade. I moved around a lot not finding much satisfaction or success in the field. I spent a year with the IRS as an agent and then worked in several public accounting firms doing audits and taxes. I found I had to work very hard to compensate for a background which had been not only devoid of anything remotely connected to business but lacking in even basic economic skills. I had never thought about what to do with money only what to do without it.

I don't know where my motivation or interest in education came from, not my parents; they took absolutely no interest in my schooling,(in fact, neither did anyone, teachers, or relatives). Nobody said a word when I dropped out of high school after my junior year. My parents had only a grammar school education from small rural schools in the west of Ireland, education, and progress in the manner of a middle-class lifestyle was beyond their mindset and backgrounds. They had lived through the Great Depression and survival, not success, was the name of the game for them and many other people of that era. The idea was to stop any slide into financial oblivion not to make progress.

Dropping out of high school was a deep personal failure for me. I could handle the curricula, but I was totally out of sync with my peers. I had no friends, ate lunch alone and wandered around the halls like a lonely ghost. I was acutely sensitive of my isolation and aware of their recognition of it too. My solitary childhood caught up with me, I had no social skills and was afraid of the other kids. After dropping out, I connected with my brother's friends. He was adept socially, although his friends weren't of the best quality. I relied on him for friends. We began drinking in alleys and our backyard. My brother, who was good at it, and a couple of other guys liked to fight when high, (I was a quiet, morose drunk) and we began to get in trouble. I did little fighting, but I was there. (The altar boy turned delinquent.)

They arrested us a few times and we finally spent two weeks in the county jail; the judge wanted to teach us a *lesson*. I woke up in my cell one morning to find an older guy going through my clothes: He slapped me and I hit him a good shot which busted his lip. We fought two more times, and I gave it up and took a dive because I was afraid what would happen if I won. I had visions of a gang beating or a knife in my back. It was last time I was in trouble with the law except for rare traffic tickets. However, it haunted me when getting into the Army and later the IRS. The record is now expunged due to my age at the time.

I was lucky to survive. I remember coming home one very cold, snowy Chicago early morning. Clark Street deserted, and the snow swirled around me as I lurched toward home literally bouncing off buildings and then parked cars as I staggered forward. About two blocks from home, I saw this white bundle of snow on the street. It was so tempting. Exhausted, I lay down in it as if it were a soft white pillow and in seconds I was asleep. Then, abruptly, someone was shaking my shoulder. I looked up, and a man stood there "You can't do that.", he said and moved on. Reluctantly, I got up and shook off the snow and made it home. He saved my life. I had heard of an Irish cousin who died that way.

Another time, I was stumbling up the stairs to our third-floor flat. I was walking up the last six stairs from a landing to the porch when suddenly I started walking down the stairs one-by-one, backwards. When I hit the rail, I hung there, horizontal for a few seconds, and fell to the ground almost three stories below. I missed an iron sewer by inches. Fortunately, it was dirt, and I was completely relaxed. I lay there stunned for a few minutes trying to figure out what happened to me then I got up and walked up the stairs, more sober now, to the flat and my bed. The next day I forgot all about it. I didn't care too much whether I lived or died. I didn't believe anyone gave a fuck about me and I was feeling the same way. I remember I used to almost unconsciously hum this little tune from a blues song," nobody loves me, nobody seems to care". It was a self-destructive time.

We weren't good sons. We could have done more to help our struggling mother rather than worrying her about our drinking and fighting. I did what she asked, but she didn't ask much. I always worked and gave money, but that was about it. I worked on shipping docks, factories, and printing companies. The poverty was always there; I got a good job at a railroad but quit after a couple of weeks when I heard them talking about how I dressed and how poor the family must be. There was an element of pity in the conversation that hurt me. At 20 I realized I was at a dead end with my fellow misfits and my life on the streets and I volunteered for the draft. That was the most important move I ever made in my life.

I did two years in the Army, got away from the streets, got the GI Bill, a lot of good food and some discipline. I was in bad shape when I went in and basic was hard and the Missouri winter cruel. I remember how cold the butt of the M-1 rifle was when we marched. I caught the flu and missed some training. Marching with a bunch of young raw recruits, I wondered how we ever won wars although later, I saw older seasoned vets their demeanor showed me how we did. They had that look and ambiance of men who had been in war and knew what it was like. I went to Fort Sill, Oklahoma, where I was a clerk-typist (I had learned to type in high school). Later I went to the Pentagon as a courier.

One week I delivered mail to offices in the Pentagon and the next week I had a civilian driver who took me to the State Department, the White House and other government agencies. They classified me to handle "secret" mail, however, I used to read it in the back seat of the car between stops and it was mundane, a guy wanting his dishonorable discharge changed and stuff like that. I was just great duty and not much soldiering. I got along casually with the other guys in the barracks. They called our four-man bunk room the "pit" and we failed inspections regularly.

I remember the guys in our room. Tommy, a small, insecure guy from Boston who liked to drink, Cohen, an overweight Jew from New York City, as neurotic as hell but deep down not a bad guy, and Earl from Mississippi who had one glass eye. I could never figure out which one was real. One evening, for no apparent reason, he sat on a bunk by me and told me in a low, sincere voice, how he and some other guys had murdered someone down there. I was speechless by this confession. Some weeks later, I was going up the stairs to the Orderly Room when he came down flanked by two military policemen, "They got me Hugh," he said rather dramatically. That was the last I saw of poor Earl.

Upon discharge, I came home to nothing. My mother had given up the Clark Street flat, which made much sense and lived where she worked as a domestic. So I got an apartment and started living with her. I felt the obligation to do something for her to make up for my delinquent years. I started night school and a round of jobs clerking. Weekends I would go to a local bar where a lot of my old classmates and one of my former misfits hung around Art Cresham's Inn. Art's had a long bar that curved at the end (my favorite place), a colorful juke box, a 26 girl and a pool table, upstairs he had rented out rooms.

It could have been in an Eugene O'Neil play, colorful as hell with a vast array of characters, frequent fights, and lots of drinking. Art was an orphan from a local Catholic orphanage, as were some other guys. He had red hair and a pronounced limp which didn't impede him from moving swiftly from one customer to another behind a big bar serving up steins. He had the Irish gift of bullshit and never lacked for conversational overtures. My father and brother hung around another bar in the neighborhood where my father got drunk and my brother would periodically beat the shit out of somebody.

There were college students, but mostly neighborhood types, a smiling guy running futility for alderman, a new cop, a Latino motorman given to wild tales, a financial adviser, a court reporter, some laborers, always a few unemployed, and a few mentally disturbed types. And some, I had no idea of what they did. There was a guy named Wally Johnson, lithe, strong build, crew cut, eyes full of hostility who was one of the best barroom fighters I have ever seen, His hate made him so. He had the habit of going over to the Southern Inn after Art's closed for the night, where he would beat the shit out of some Southerner.

One night they were waiting for him with baseball bats and sent him and two friends to the hospital one a likable young bartender with them was killed. They diagnosed Wally as a paranoid schizophrenic and committed him. It was rough stuff even for Art's. While I would load up on beer on a Friday night and often closed the bar at 2am. I didn't drink during the week. I knew there was a better life, but I didn't know how to get there. I made two abortive attempts joining a group at night school and a church social but that was it.

In my accounting jobs, everything was new to me. When the tax season came, I would take whatever return came my way no matter how complicated and somehow got it done. I was reading in the tax books all the time, breaks, and lunch periods. I would dig out the prior year's return and see how it was done and then just do it. It was learn as you go and I got very good at doing that. I figured I would compensate with an energetic effort for what I lacked in knowledge. At first I made mistakes, but I honed my skills to where some partners only wanted to use me because I was such a prodigious producer. I decided I liked taxes better than auditing, (words rather than numbers) then becoming a federal tax manager at a medium-sized corporation a subsidiary of a large conglomerate on Chicago's north-side in the Seventies.

During my tenure in the corporate world, I blew the whistle twice on corporations I believed were involved in financial wrong-doing. In one case I was right, in the other nothing developed and I may have been wrong in my interpretation. I had overheard the accountant talking about "stonewalling the IRS" on a foreign tax deduction and I had passed it on to the IRS auditors but in retrospect I think he was just smart talking and there was no real fraud.

The other time I was working at a cab company as a supervisor of sorts. I found some correspondence about a devious deduction the company was taking and an allusion as how to deal with the IRS. I copied it and sent it to them. An agent came in, he smiled as he saw me but said nothing. I don't know the outcome of that whistleblowing, but I think it struck home. I was at an art opening reception about two years later and the president of the company was next to me picking up some goodies off a table and I felt like whispering in his ear about what I had done. I must have been drinking too much wine.

One of my jobs there and I hated it was to apply liens to driver's checks. They would come in the office and leave with 15% deducted from their check, not a pleasant scene. Most took it in stride being used to the ritual. One fat, black guy came in and laid a gun on the desk. At first, I interpreted it as a threat but carried on as usual, then we started bullshitting about football and he told me he had played in high school. It ended nicely, he picked up the gun and left. Another tall, well built black man came in and I asked him his name, "Doris", he said. I wasn't sure if I heard it right and he repeated "Doris,". I wasn't about to make any jokes but I did say "unusual name for a man." He answered matter-of-factly, "It's from the Bible," he said. I sat imaging what it must have been like for him growing up. Doris left without another word.

I had no real reservations about blowing the whistle on corporations I've thought were wrong-doing. I've never felt that an employer bought my principles when he hired me; I've never thought any sense of "loyalty" precluded my doing the right thing and expecting them to do the same. I definitely felt they had no right to expect me to do something wrong for them and I just would not do it. I would not be a corporate lackey.

Besides, I always thought it somewhat puzzling that a corporation which has no compassion in laying off employees with many years of service somehow feels employees owe them dog-like loyalty because they gave them a check for their services over the years. This loyalty to the company attitude might go back to the days of feudalism with the lord demanding a similar loyalty from serfs because he was a lord, and they were on his turf. In my mind, an employer bought my time and skills not my integrity. I believe a person should be loyal, foremost to themselves, to their values, not to some corporate entity.

Over the years I had moved, incrementally, from what was an inherited conservative Democratic political philosophy to a more liberal one (although I don't always vote Democratic I am cataloged as an "unaffiliated", I do, 95% of the time. In the Seventies I did precinct work for the Independent Precinct Organization, trying to challenge the entrenched and often corrupt Daley Democratic machine.

I spent weeks going through a north-side lakefront neighborhood full of three to twelve story apartment buildings knocking on doors and passing out literature for a candidate I knew didn't have a chance. I was surprised how trusting people were, one pretty young woman let me into her apartment in her nightgown, having gotten out of a tossed up couch bed in the living room to answer the door. "I probably shouldn't have done that she said", I nodded. I completed the futile canvasing effort. The Don Quixote in me was expressing itself again.

I bumped into the local Daley machine guy one day doing canvas work, "Who are you?" he demanded to know, like I was an intruder into his territory, I told him, he said nothing and walked off. Two weeks later, I was changing clothes buying some pants in a clothing store and found a wallet on the floor. It had a badge in it. The owner was some kind of deputy bailiff. I called the number in it and he came right over. It was him, the machine guy. He was so grateful he bought me a box of expensive cigars. Losing a badge is almost as bad as losing a gun, hard to live down for these guys.

I was active in community groups and volunteered with small non-profit groups. I prepared free tax returns at libraries and half-way houses for lower-income people. (not pure altruism, it makes me feel good to do good). Although I was moving up toward middle management, I was not comfortable in the corporate world. I had this need to do more than just make money for an organization. I felt stifled by corporate values and work: preparing financial statements, attending meetings and pretending to care about the company's "bottom line" made me feel like a con man. I was faking it. Not that I couldn't see some worth in what they were doing; We need the products of business it was just that I had a different priority of values. I was working for business during the day and often against it at night. Suffering from a kind of schizophrenia of values, I decided in the late Seventies to drop out of corporate life to do consulting with non-profit organizations.

I found work with community groups, an academic union, arts organizations, and some liberal political activist centers. I enjoyed my consulting work with non-profits although I barely made a living; it was non-profit for me too. My "clients" included the Citizen Labor Energy Coalition, a then influential activist group coalesced around the "energy crisis" and supported by celebrities such as Paul Newman; the Midwest Academy, an important and unique activist training center, which trained hundreds of activists in the noted Saul Alinsky Chicago style of organizing for political change; a prominent Socialist periodical called "In These Times"; the Chicago Artists Coalition and the United Food and Commercial Workers local union. I liked the people in the groups I worked with, they were dedicated, intelligent and dynamic. Their missions were noble and interesting. I got to know some players and most of the activist groups in the Chicago area. I would never return to the corporate world and I never regretted leaving it.

CHAPTER THREE:
SWEET HOME CHICAGO

The dearest ones of time, the strongest friends for the soul - BOOKS
- Emily Dickinson

I was apprehensive about going to the International's convention in 1986. Although the city's gangster reputation is exaggerated and somewhat of a caricature things "happen" in Chicago. A chilling example: the episode wherein a gang of bold, but foolish burglars robbed Tony Arcardo's, the Outfit's boss's mansion in River Forest while he was in Palm Springs. Within a year they found all seven members of the gang dead with their throats cut, the Italian among them castrated while another thief had his face blow-torched. Afterwards, the two men who had done the hits turned up dead. The bosses were covering their murderous tracks.

If fear is the mother of respect, then the traditional ability of the Mob to kill at will and get away with it in Chicago commands respect, at least for that ability if not for the morality of it. I kept a very low profile at the convention and didn't use the name tag they gave me. I stayed in the background and helped with the setup and registration but had no direct contact with the registrants. I attended a few informal meetings, but I avoided everything else. I wanted to be as anonymous as possible and called on my childhood skill at being inconspicuous.

I skipped parties and most personal contacts spending a good deal of time in my hotel room. Hanley's son got married during the convention, and they had a big party. I was very tempted to go to see who would show up; I was sure everybody "connected ", whether wiseguys, politicians, or clergy, who could discreetly attend would be there, but I decided not to attend because of the suspicions I had triggered. Also, I sensed some people avoiding me, distancing themselves from someone who might be trouble. I walked up to Massey in the Hilton lobby, "How you doing Frank?" "Okay,"' he said, and he glided away without another word.

I was at lunch in a restaurant near the hotel that day when a group of men from the notorious Atlantic City local arrived and sat across the aisle from my booth. They could have been the supporting cast of a Martin Scorsese film (life imitating art), dark and sinister looking, very well-dressed with alert, hostile eyes. I began to wonder how much they knew about *me*. Could the word be out on me as a spy? Then I wondered whether I was getting somewhat paranoid. This kind of thinking became common for me in time. I was never sure what was real or what might be my hyper-vigilant imagination in certain situations. I avoided looking at them, finished my lunch, and left.

I got to visit my mother who lived up on the north side in a senior citizen's high-rise apartment near Lincoln park that I had arranged for her to live in. We would settle into a familiar, often redundant, pattern of conversation with her doing most of the talking. Usually it revolved around relatives, friends, people who lived in the building and sometimes old stories I had heard many times before. Our traditional way of relating, her talking, me listening. Like most mothers, she would find it obligatory to feed me when I came and I would feel the need to buy a bunch of groceries for her. I told her nothing of my union intrigue. I would give her a few general details of my work; She would ask me if I liked my job and I would nod and just say "Yes, I do."

She seemed content, had contact with my suburban sister and brother in Georgia and her sister and brother along with others. She didn't make much contact with the "old people" in the building, kept to herself as she had most of her life focusing on a small group of relatives and friends. She corresponded with Sally, a girl she had known since elementary school for over seventy-five years. As kids we taught her to smoke, a habit, unfortunately she never gave it up, but then again, never caused her any serious illness, odd because she was TB survivor. We called her "Mud", nothing derogatory meant, just a nickname that stuck that she liked.

When I return to Chicago, as soon as my feet hit the streets, I am transformed the way an animal is when it returns to its native habitat. I am home! Immediately comfortable, confident the way someone is in a familiar environment and energized with the excitement of rediscovery. When I lived in the city, I was all over it and had an intimate knowledge of the city that a taxicab driver would envy. I knew the culture, the history, the good neighborhoods, and the bad ones, the galleries, the theatres, the good cheap restaurants, and the free parking spots.

I would go for a short walk and walk miles just soaking up the sights and sounds, the rhythm and movement of the city. The people, an amazing collective, both of diverse, distinctive individuals and almost stereotyped habituates imprinted with the city's personality. I loved its power and intensity and hated its congestion and politics. The city still has a deep hold on my psyche. On one trip, I walked 15 miles the first day I was there, soaking up the feel of the city. I wound up with bandages on my blisters but continued walking (although not as much).

I always do a pilgrimage to my old neighborhood when I go back to Chicago. All but two of the storefronts businesses in my neighborhood have been replaced by others over the decades and the newsstand is gone, (the corner has never seemed "right" to me without it). Once there were a tavern and a nightclub, a funeral home, an antique shop, a large movie theater, a tailor, a phone company office, a little restaurant, and large old apartment building in half a block. Only the animal hospital and Paris Inn had survived the decades and the Paris Inn (which was actually Chinese), where my mother took us once on our only dinner out as kids, after an argument with my father over another empty payday, (he claimed some men had mugged him).

My mother put on her coat and gathered us kids. I remember him crying in the kitchen sink and I walked over and asked him, "What's wrong, Daddy?" My mother became angry "Stay with him if you want", I left with her, but I didn't like the way she put the choice. I had chop suey for the first time in my life and I also saw my first movie that evening. I still remember the ending because it had a trailer at the end of the movie asking people not to reveal the ending. The neighborhood had recycled its storefronts, remodeled some buildings and changed business signs but there were still the streets and buildings which stood like ancient paths and caverns that outlived their travelers and occupants. I have a photo of the street I grew up on my "Chicago" wall in the living room with some other Chicago memorabilia.

Our old turn of the century six flat building had been obliterated and replaced with a four-story brick parking lot with a large blatant neon sign, "Century parking Lot." The first thought that occurred to me was they had accomplished what we never did; they had gotten rid of the cockroaches by cementing them over. I stood there on the street somewhat disorientated trying to restore the image of the old building I had grown up in. It took a few minutes for me to recreate it in my mind: the decaying old three-story brick six flat building with the fading "Aetna State Bank" advertisement painted on one side of it and the large cluttered hardware store on the first floor. Quinn's Hardware, a Clark Street fixture. A tarred road right next to the building along with "Clark's Boiler Repair Shop" which did a lot of banging and clanging during the work week

Clark Street is famous in Chicago for Wrigley Field and the St. Valentine's Day Massacre. It runs from the Evanston border, 7600 north to Cermak Road, 2200 south, a distance of 98 blocks. There were blocks of stores north of our flat and then it deteriorated to run-down stores and girlie movie machines, bordered up stores, some homeless until it reached Clark and Division which was a gay hangout, notorious in those days, and haunted by the police. Further north a string of strip joints and then, novel for the time, a Puerto Rican barrio, on to downtown, offices, restaurants, some shops, and City Hall. Then and out to the once fashionable near south side, now ignored except for a historic building or mansion.

A good way to get a sense of Chicago is to get on the Clark streetcar at Howard and take it to the end of the line. The other is to ride the "EL" trains for a second story view of the city neighborhoods, good and bad, running past back porches of rented homes, commercial buildings, innumerable streets. You'll see the sad slums, the prison-like projects, the dark side of Chicago. You can ride the "EL" north, south and west in Chicago, it drops to street level going out in those directions. Our east side is mostly Lake Michigan.

Quinn, who owned the building, was a dour old Irishman, who wasn't too happy with us as tenants (we were usually three months late on the rent although he always got it). There was always a group of old country

Irishmen chewing tobacco and bullshitting in the store. One had to walk carefully along the floor to avoid all the spit tobacco. Nobody hit the spittoon. The building itself a run-down affair, with a rotting back porch and stairs, fading red brick paint and an erratic heating system (the radiators sang a shrill song and gave off a hiss of steam when they heated).

We had a large backyard littered with debris and a small red shed where Chubby, our dog got trapped between the wall of the Century Theatre and the back of the shed and died. She disappeared, but when there was a fire in the little shed firemen chopped it up and found Chubby. We buried her in a solemn ceremony in the backyard. She was 12 years old, a loner and as far as I know, a virgin.

I walked over to the church. It was saddened to see the church charred and badly damaged; it had suffered a serious fire, (I thought of the candles and vigil lights right away). They tore it down afterwards, and they sold the entire property including the school to a neighboring hospital. I was angry, sad and somewhat unsettled. The convent now an apartment building. These places were part of my life and identity, places that somehow I unconsciously believed would always be there. Now they disappeared without a trace of their history, meaning or existence, or my relationship with them. This glimpse into the transitory nature of life, including my mortality, disturbed me. I tried to console myself with cliches about the inevitability of change in life but it didn't dispel my mood. I can still get unhappy about it.

I had lunch with a former girlfriend in a restaurant at Marshall Fields'. We reminisced about our earlier dating days and talked about mutual friends. A public school teacher who could never figure out whether she was pretty, (nor could I) She hinted she felt the need for a "companion." I ignored the comment prompting a subsequent observation obliquely implying I was kind of dense. I ignored that one too since acknowledging it would have led to a discussion on the first comment. But I liked having the connection despite the emotional undercurrents and I enjoyed visiting the city, a place I will always consider home, no matter where else I go or how long I live there. When I find someone from Chicago I corner him/her and talk about the city until they manage to escape. In short, I am still homesick.

It's been 34 years now and I still dream about the city. I'm on the "EL" platform waiting for a train, driving Lake Shore Drive, driving through the old "S" curve, (whose view of Michigan Avenue at that point was what one architectural critic called "the greatest panorama in the Western World"). Or I'm walking around the Loop, or back in the old flat on the beat-up furniture, maybe up on the corner by the newsstand. In real life, I zoom in on any news about the city on Google or the papers and listen to the local NPR station, WBEZ at times.

I get books from the university library on Chicago. I keep up with politics and get back there every couple of years. I don't understand people who can blow off their old homes like just another stop on the journey of life. For me, your former home is primal, as much a part of you as your bones, indelibly imprinted for a lifetime. I understand salmon and their deep need to return to their spawning grounds.

Our flat located only eight blocks from Wrigley Field. I knew the Cub's lineup, batting averages, and pitcher stats by heart. I can still recite some of it. I root for the Cubs, Bulls and Bears although my interest and time are limited to watching a few games and checking the standings weekly. I do the playoffs. I watched and celebrated the 2016 World Series although I believe the Cubs lost something too, maybe the fans sympathy and fondness for a perennial loser which suddenly becomes a winner. If accepting loss is a virtue we Cubs fans are sports saints.

The proposed slate of officers at the 1986 convention, including Ed Hanley, elected, as they had been for 15 years, without opposition, "by acclamation" as the union's propagandist newsletter would describe it. It was all pro-forma, scripted, a done deal, no one raised issues or objections. The speeches trite but applauded. Beefy Sergeant-At-Arms were there to keep people in line but they rarely ran into problems. I remember Grogan, dressed to the teeth in an expensive suit, standing at the door to the convention hall smoking a cigar and watching with a big self-satisfied smile on his face. Everything going according to plan. The delegates understood what their role required and followed the script faithfully.

A post-election celebration dinner had drinks and hors d'oeuvres in a separate suite prior to the dinner. The trappings were like a scene from a Fellini movie with expensive scotch and bourbon being poured by waiters in tuxedos and black ties whose tip cups overflowed with bills. Big tipping the union waiters was mandatory for the delegates, part of the show, and nobody dared put any change in the tip cups. A waiter's dream. They lined the tables with perch, rich pastries, plates of brie, a selection of marinated vegetables, caviar, dips of various kinds and rich looking delectables I could not identify. The conversation and drinking became intense. The union being in the business of servicing parties knew how to throw one.

I sat alone, had two quick scotches and some perch, then disappeared into the elevator up to my room. I felt this powerful, lonely alienation from the life around me. I wondered if I were the only one sitting alone in his room, dismayed and disgusted by the event taking place 10 floors below. I had doubts: How could I be right about this and everybody else wrong? Maybe this was just the way things happened in life; Maybe this was the way they played the game, and I didn't know how to play it. Was I just naive? Still being too good? The two scotches put me to sleep.

Wayne Newton, a favorite of the union, performed for the delegates, staff, and guests at a lavish dinner. "You missed all the fun," a female employee said to me the next day. (Yeah, I thought, and I also missed getting myself in trouble too). As we folded up our chairs, took down the registration tables and packed our boxes, Ed Hanley came over and sat in a large red chair about 45 feet from me. He stared hard at me. I continued a humorous banter with one secretary, all the while aware of his stare. After some minutes he got up and left. I understood. He wanted me to understand that he knew. Much, much later I learned he told Leavitt, "Okay, he can stay but you're responsible for him." Big mistake.

It relieved me when I started on the road with the new check-off program and started working with the locals. The trip gave me a break from the tension and scrutiny I sensed at the International. I began a grueling odyssey of travel that would last six years: no home, no apartment, no setting. My first stop, Cincinnati, and I started a pattern of working that lasted through my time with the union: working until late in the evening, finding a place to eat and then going back to the motel or hotel. A very lonely life but having always been something of a loner I had a capacity for loneliness that most people do not have, (nor want). I'd tell people that if I got food, some exercise, and books I could do solitary confinement. Hopefully, I'll never have to prove that boast.

I never got into the Godfather, Sopranos, etc. I thought Scorsese's "Mean Streets" was okay but the film, I thought caught the real Mafia best is Casavette's "Mikey and Nicky" with him and Peter Falk playing two minor league hoods. Most of the Mob are run-of-the-mill, fucked up guys not the slick, well-dressed Mafia types you see in movies, half of them hardly earn a living. Grogan, one time described them, smiling as he said "They're always scheming Hughie, always scheming". Incidentally Scorsese's "The Irishman" is fiction not fact. FBI agents say calling Sheeran Hoffa's killer is preposterous, even criminals knowledgeable about the crime, agree with that assessment. Scorsese is not doing truth a favor with this film in my opinion.

Traveling, I would read a book or watch a little TV, the news, public television, or an NBA game if in season, and then go to bed. I remember I sat watching a Bulls playoff game at the local in Seattle. I decided to get something to eat at a Thai restaurant I had been to before. They had one to five stars for the strength of hot spicy. I had three stars the last time I ate there and decided I could handle five. After I ordered, I saw the waiter and two others having a conference and looking at me. I took the meal t the local and devoured it, no problem but two days later I paid the price, my stomach revolted and I hit the toilet many times. A culinary learning experience. I got library cards in some locations where I knew I would be for a while and continued to feed my reading addiction, (These days I go through an average of 250-300 books a year, an unrecovered, unrepentant biblioholic. I should join an addiction support group). I do it, not page by page necessarily, but I try to do each one justice. I feel guilty if I don't.

It was books and film that first implemented the idea that one could change things. I remember "The Jungle" and how Upton Sinclair brought attention to the terrible working conditions in the Chicago stockyards, which resulted in important legislation. And Jacob Riis's poignant photographs of poverty in New York City. Old movies such as "To Kill a Mockingbird", "Knock on Any Door", Matewan, Wiseman's documentaries: "Welfare", "Titicut Follies". Books like Harrington's "The Other America". The lives of Robert Kennedy, Martin Luther King, Oscar Romero, Cesar Chavez, Ralph Nader and so many more who fed into my mind, memory, and emotions.

Reading has been my salvation. I could not honestly have lived without it or wanted to. If I had to choose between sex and reading, I would choose the latter. I didn't start reading seriously until my twenties when taking liberal arts courses. I became addicted. I often have two dozen or more books out from 2 to 3 different libraries. One time I returned 40 books out of my car's trunk to the Chicago Public Library, took them an hour and a half to work out the fines totaling $75, (pre-computer days). I am in a library at least once a week. I pay my fines for late returns or lost books without regrets. I believe the library is the world's greatest bargain and one of its most important institutions. (One librarian called me a "library bum," jokingly...I hope) I bring them chocolate with every visit which they love and will forgive anything.

I found out, rather disappointingly that, rather than reading literary gems, they read mysteries and science fiction. I don't know where it came from, but I had, considering my background and with little guidance, surprisingly good taste in what I read. I developed a real knowledge of literature in general, however, mostly contemporary works, there are some de rigueur classics I have never read. I had passed over literature as a career vocation but somehow we had found each other anyhow and I never let go. I don't consider myself an intellectual but more likely someone with intellectual aspirations and something of a literary poseur. But what the hell, I love it.

It comes down to living life or reading about it or reading it or writing about it. I try, albeit unsuccessfully, to balance things out. I started to pick up books on the Mafia and labor unions. Most of the books talked about the Mafia and the Teamsters, and I only found occasional allusions to HEREIU. But I started building a background of knowledge on organized crime influence in unions. It wasn't pretty, money, and murder, and rank exploitation of the members. Their methods are primitive, brutal, but effective. And the fact is it doesn't take much to scare people.

I avoided motel and hotel bars, the usual social outlet on the road. Beyond having lunch with the officers and staff of the locals occasionally, I had little other social contact with them. They had their lives to live, and I didn't think I had the right to impose any social demands on them. Besides, I didn't know who to trust. I stayed in a wide variety of motels and hotels and learned to dislike them intensely. The motels deadening in their similarity: the same sprayed odor seemed to heighten the banality of the room to me; the ubiquitous cable television and remote with TV guide on top of it; the phone with a number for the motel operator and wake-up calls; the Bible in the dresser drawer; maybe a tacky landscape picture on the wall and the wrapped soap, a little bottle of cologne or shampoo to use or take as a souvenir.

The rooms to me, like voluntary jail cells, were places to sleep, shower, and forget as quickly as possible. In the morning there was the much advertised "American plan" free breakfast, the plan usually consisting of some stale generic coffee, diluted orange juice and a gooey pastry. They told me to "stay union" and I did that as best I could but sometimes it wasn't practical or possible so too often I found myself in a Motel Six, Best Western, Days Inn, Quality Inn, etc. The motels stood in strips which I used to call "anywhere USA" because one could see in these strips the almost identical business inhabitants. There would be Travelodge, Red Roof Inn, Holiday Inn, Exon, Wendy's. Econo Lodge, Howard Johnson, Burger King, Pizza Hut; the same signs, the same deja vu architecture.

There was the same food, anywhere in any town in the country, only the faces of the workers were different, (although the patter always the same, "Hope you enjoyed your stay", "Have a nice day", "Come back and see us" etc., etc). You wonder about the deterioration of architecture and creativity in America when they turn out these banal cookie-cutter buildings for the sake of profit and functionality. I found that travel can be as stifling as it can be broadening.

On Sundays, I would go to the local Unitarian Fellowship. Despite their relatively small numbers (roughly 230,000 nationwide then) I found a Fellowship in just about every place I went. I claim, rightly or wrongly the lay record for the number of Unitarian Fellowships I have attended, over 150 including the unique "First Existentialist Unitarian Congregation of Atlanta" which still exists. Although Unitarianism embraces all religious approaches: Buddhist, Theist, Atheist, Humanist, etc. The Humanistic philosophy in Unitarianism had the strongest appeal for me. Humanism dispensed with theology, replacing religious dogma with interrelationship values: emphasizing integrity, courage, responsibility, tolerance, compassion, and social justice. Most important to me was the recognition of each individual's innate *worth* as a human being paramount in Unitarianism. I wanted and needed that sense of self worth. They emphasized one's search for truth and meaning among their principles. I never joined but was always a "friend" and I tried to be a good one.

I loaded up on related groups, the local Unitarian Fellowship, the Ethical Humanist Society, a member of the American Ethical Union, small national group dedicated to ethical living without a creed or theology. I was finding like-minded people, and I needed that. I still hangout, at the local Ethical Humanist Society and more regularly at the local Unitarian Fellowship. Tolerant, thoughtful, creative, sincere, informed, dedicated people. I can't say enough how constantly impressed I am with these people attuned to social injustice and how they act to correct it. Being Humanist and Atheist can be a lonely, alien role in our general society, and it is a gift to have folks like this to have as friends.

Doing the right thing out of human respect and compassion made more sense than doing it because one receive commandments to do it by a deity or because one is rewarded with a heaven or punished with a hell if one fails. (I had moved a long way from my altar boy days, sometimes I wonder how that twelve-year-old would look at me now, I don't think he would understand me). The golden rule, "Do unto others as you would have them do unto you", was profound and practical in its simplicity. These Humanist values had a deep resonance for me and provided me with the reinforcement of the personal values I needed to sustain my efforts to work for social justice.

I've never liked cheaters. Maybe we all cheat a little but there are those who make it a lifestyle., especially those with money. When I worked for the IRS as a Revenue Agent, I found myself tough on those types of cheaters. I worked the badlands of Chicago, the south and west side, large gray sad pockets of poverty filled with boarded-up shops, projects or slums, vacant lots with broken liquor bottles, debris, and weeds. The first time I drove out there I sat in my car for five minutes before I got out to do my job. The people understood what I was doing there; Sometimes a bottle would come flying out of a project window and crash in the street near me. People glared at me. The gang members didn't like it. I heard one guy yell out: "What's that white MF doing down here?" The people figured it was bad enough we put them in the ghetto and now we should stay the hell out of it. Most figured I was "the Man" and didn't mess with me.

I also covered some of the more exclusive Lake Shore Drive territory, which, as the name implies, ran along Lake Michigan. One day I would be in the notorious Cabrini-Green housing projects and the next in a fashionable Lake Shore suite. I didn't like slapping liens on the paychecks of poor working-class people but I relished doing it to some business people and affluent types who didn't want to pay any taxes and played every game possible to avoid them. I was dedicated in my efforts to nail them. One time I went to a downtown hotel to serve a subpoena on former heavyweight champion Ingemar Johansson, fortunately for me, perhaps he wasn't in his room.

My IRS experience gave me some investigative skills and empowered me with a sense that I could correct wrong-doing. During my time there, I was involved in picking up some taxpayers for fraud investigations. My zeal on tax cheats carried over into my professional career and I once blew the whistle on a partner in a CPA firm who I was working for during the tax season. I knew he was aggressively taking large phony deductions for wealthy clients and subtly encouraging me to do the same. I remember his smile of satisfaction as he did so, as if slipping fraud past the government was singularly rewarding to him. The whole thing a game to him.

The locals were receptive to being computerized, but wary of the motives of the International. They feared that their correspondence might be screened and their personal affairs monitored by the International if they took on a computer. I had to reassure them that this would not be technically possible since there was to be no modem connection to the International's computer. It took some convincing but most of them came around in time and developed a trust in me. That the International was paying for the equipment and training was a strong incentive for the locals to computerize. Some local people, because I was on the International staff, stayed suspicious of me. This bothered me. I didn't like being stereotyped as "one of them." I always wanted to set them straight and say, "Hey, I'm not one of them, I'm okay" but I couldn't and didn't.

Some locals walked a tightrope with the International cooperating with them when they had to but strove to maintain distance and independence. Some of them played the International well running up large deficits in their per capita tax. They knew how recklessly the International spent their money and that the ineffectiveness of the Secretary-Treasurer's office in collecting delinquent dues worked in the local's favor. But while the locals might play games with the per capita dues, there was also fear. The president of one local put it frankly when he told me, "The International can do anything it wants and I mean *anything*". He said it with a fatalistic realism that hit me.

I found a sad disenchantment in some long-time employees of some locals. I remember a conversation with a female, a veteran staff member of a local, "I used to be proud to work for the union once but now I'm ashamed to say I do". She said it with a sad regret that touched me. I wanted to tell her I always felt the same way about revealing my employment in the union but I just nodded. I cringed when people asked me where I worked and always measured their reaction when I told them, waiting for a knowing look or caustic comment. However, I found that only labor insiders knew of the union's notoriety.

I started learning the basics of union life at the locals watching the union people do their work dealing with member grievances and negotiating with employers while the office staff dealt with initiations, dues, jobs. The business agents seemed to have a tough job arbitrating endless problems between the employer and employees. I walked my first picket line, something they didn't require me to do, but I wanted to experience, it. (I've always found the chanting, "What do you want?" "Justice", "When do you want it?", "Now!" kind of stuff rather inane but I don't know any better technique either). People generally blew off the picket line and went about their business, but some would take an interest in the issue and stop and talk with us. And some would honor the picket line, a gesture which always elicited much gratitude from the strikers and raised their spirits.

I had lunch occasionally with the local's officers and got a sense of their personality and involvement in the union. Many were hardworking, decent unionists committed to their membership. Some not so, clearly going through the motions, putting their lunches on their expense account and picking up their paycheck every two weeks was their idea of working. Meanwhile, I was still being watched, this time by International auditors, who would show up at the local where I was working to keep an eye and an ear on me. I made it a point to take advantage of conversations with the local officers to say positive things about the International within the earshot of the visiting auditor. Within a few months, the visits from the auditors stopped, and I began to explore the locals with a view toward finding out any corruption at that level. I found a few.

I didn't get back in D.C. for any length of time until July when we stopped installing the program because of bugs and the programmer started cleaning them up. I felt more relaxed, sensed that I was being accepted and the intense suspicion I had experienced early on from some people was dissipating. I enjoyed being in D.C.; one of the most interesting cities I have ever experienced. It seemed everybody was doing something important. I heard interesting conversations on the Metro, (a revelation itself compared with the Chicago subway of those days, no graffiti on the walls, no banana peels or empty wine bottles on the floor or seats) from people who worked at the State Department and in other government agencies. There were embassy types whose features and dress broadcast their national origin. There were all kinds of high-ranking military on the streets, ambassadors in stretch limos, and an intriguing institute of some sort on almost every corner. It was like a huge movie set.

I also liked the European flavor of the Capital's architecture and had a hard time, early on, navigating circles (different from Chicago's neat grid layout). The omnipresent White House and Capitol building gave the city a sense of power and drama. Washington, however, seemed a place where most professional people worked but didn't live. I did some tourist things in DC: the Smithsonian, National Gallery, Hirshhorn Museum, Kennedy Center, Library of Congress (I remember Jefferson's library). But I never exploited the attractions of the city as much as I could have or should have. I would go to bookstores and cafes in Georgetown or on Connecticut Avenue when I had a little time. I was too absorbed in the affairs of the union to do much serious sightseeing. I had no social life except for an occasional single's event at the Unitarian Fellowship. I had two abortive dates, and that was about it.

One with a psychologist in her mid-forties. She had a light, carefree attitude and I could tell she was not looking for any deep connection either. We did some art galleries and she would wander off looking at other paintings (this is de rigueur with feminist type women who want to make a point they will not follow men around) it was okay by me. On the way home she said something I still think was one of the funniest lines I ever heard on a date. "You can stay at my house tonight. but we only have two beds and you'll have to sleep in the one with my nineteen-year-old daughter". It was a takeoff on the old jokes of a salesman staying at a farmer's house when his car breaks down and he has to sleep in the same room with the farmer's daughter. Maybe I have a perverse sense of humor, but I still smile when I think of her comment. As it turned out I didn't sleep with either of them. :-)

I met a blonde woman, nice figure and congenial at a Unitarian singles event and went to her apartment with her. Her living room was her bedroom, and she actually laid on her bed as she talked with me. I sat in a chair next to the bed. And she talked and talked and talked non-stop. At one point exhausted listening I stopped her and pointed it out to her. She explained how her father a sea captain who, when he returned home, didn't let her talk as a child. She was making up for it now, it almost seemed compulsive. She resumed talking. I took my leave, "You don't have to leave," she said, but any sexual motivation had left me during the monologues. In retrospect, I found it rather poignant.

CHAPTER FOUR:
I MAKE A TOUGH DECISION

To act is to be committed, to be committed is to be in danger
- James Baldwin

Things were moving along smoothly enough. Although I still had misgivings and kept my eyes and ears open, I had settled into the union culture and more comfortable working in it. And they seemed more comfortable with me. But all this changed, one morning I was in the conference room when Frank Massey, came in with his aide. The audit manager had a thick collection of papers bound with a metal clasp. He threw it on the conference table. "These guys are really smart," he said. I glanced at the reports title, "The Edge: Organized Crime, Business, and Labor Unions". The report had a U. S. Senate letterhead. I could barely restrain myself from asking him if I might read it. Instead, I made a mental note of the title and knew I had to get it.

I was still working evenings, drinking multiple cups of coffee every day. The secretary who ordered the coffee came down one day and wondered out loud why the coffee consumption had gone up so dramatically. I smiled and shrugged my shoulders. I became adept at wandering through the offices and knowing who was and wasn't there. I knew who had a habit of working late to catch a train or waiting an hour to beat the traffic. I knew who drove and who took public transportation. I knew who was in or out of town. My seat in the basement had a view of the rear door which led to the underground parking garage so I could see people come and go with ease. I was getting ready to explore again, and I had a front-row seat.

Then one evening walking through the second-floor hallway I saw a report on a chair in an office, I got excited. I went quickly in and flipped it over; It was *the* report. I stuck in under my arm and then, once downstairs, put it into my briefcase and took off. I started reading the report at dinner and read it and reread into the night. The report by a Senate Subcommittee which held several hearings on organized crime influence in unions in 1983. The report on HEREIU began with a quote from Paul Castellano, who,until John Gotti assassinated him in 1985, was head of the New York Gambino family. Castellano, referring to the International, says on a wiretap, "Somebody else owns the International". He was referring to the Chicago Outfit and Tony Arcardo.

The report stated that the International "has a documented relationship with the Chicago "Outfit" of La Cosa Nostra at the International level and subject to the influence of the New York Gambino, Colombo families, and Philadelphia La Cost Nostra at the local level". The report gave a brief history of the union and its struggle with organized crime elements. This led to periodic investigations by government including Thomas Dewey in New York in 1937; the Kefauver Committee in 1950 and the McClellan Committee in 1958. That report told of Accardo taking the Fifth Amendment against self-incrimination before the McClellan Committee.

In the Twenties the Mob discovered that unions, which began organizing in the late Nineteenth Century, had grown into a lucrative target not only for their assets but for the ability their control gave hoodlums to extort protection money from businesses. Threatening strikes, cutting off supplies and services, picketing, and violence were effective tools and techniques in convincing recalcitrant owners to contribute to their "protectors". They took over unions like the Movie Projectionist Union, the Electrical Workers Union, the Cleaners and Dyers Union, and the Taxi Drivers Union. By the end of the Twenties, the Mob controlled over two-thirds of the city's unions and wanted more.

The Mob's move into control of HEREIU,s Chicago's locals was anything but subtle. In 1935 Frank, (the Enforcer) Nitti of the Capone Mob and George McLane, the secretary of Local 278 of the Chicago Bartenders Union, met in a Clark Street restaurant. Nitti wanted to put one of his men into the local. The dialogue might have come from a

Hollywood scriptwriter: Mr. McLane stayed reluctant until Nitti said, "We want no more playing around. If you don't do what we say, you will get shot in the head". He then asked Mc Lane how he thought his wife would look in black (a vision that caused Mr. McLane to quickly change his mind). The Mob later failed to elect Mr. McLane as President of the International union. However, the Mob was in the union for keeps. Joey Aiuppa, a gunman for Capone was listed on Local 450's application to the International for a charter. He had no problem getting it.

The report told the history about Mob control of Locals 278 and 450 in Chicago and related testimony from an informer, Joseph Hauser, who said that Ed Hanley was hand-picked by Tony Arcardo for the International presidency and that "Aiuppa, (an Outfit under-boss) and Arcardo continued "to exert great influence over the union and its president, Ed Hanley." Hanley started as a business agent for Local 450 in 1957, became secretary-treasurer of Local 278 in 1964, following the murder of the previous secretary-treasurer. He became President of International in 1973. The payroll of the union quadrupled and Hanley doubled his salary in one year. Union assets dropped over 40% from 21 million to 12 million in 4 years and six million dollars funneled into three loans to private developers, one of whom, Morris Shenker had organized crime ties.

The Subcommittee found that the salaries and "allowances" including unlimited expense accounts, lifetime compensation contracts, and lucrative pensions sent expenses soaring seven fold in ten years. A former Secretary-Treasurer, John Gibson continued to receive his lifetime salary, pension, a leased car and expense account after his release from prison serving four months for embezzling union funds and being barred from holding a union office. Perversely, the International honored him by making him "Secretary Emeritus". That one really got me.

The Subcommittee commented on Jackie Presser and Ralph Natale and other Mob connected type who worked as organizers for the union. (Hanley said he didn't care who they were "As long as they did the job"). Hanley increased the number of "organizers" from twenty to over a hundred after his assumption of power over the union playing the Chicago patronage game. The Subcommittee expressed its concern over the manner in which Hanley centralized authority, merged welfare and pension funds and dominated local unions through mergers, trusteeships, and transfers. They merged dissenting unions into larger loyal locals submerging dissent. Hanley affected 136 mergers from 1973 to 1984. He also moved 16 pension funds and 35 welfare funds under International Control.

Hanley took the Fifth Amendment 34 times before the Subcommittee refusing to answer even basic questions such as his union title. Senator Warren Rudman called his refusal to testify "the height of arrogance." Hanley made one statement: "I have never been associated with any person known to be members of an organized crime family." This from a guy who was a brother-in-law and uncle to two notorious Chicago Mob figures: the Calabreses, father and son. In a deja vu moment, Godfather Arcardo took the Fifth as he had done 25 years before in front the McClellen Committee.

Hanley's refusal to testify violated the AFL-CIO canon of ethical behavior, which allows officials to take the Fifth but requires them to resign their position if they do. The AFL-CIO, however, ignored this act as it has traditionally chosen to ignore labor corruption in its ranks, an attitude that seriously eroded its public image and had to hurt organizing efforts. Hanley had a seat on the AFL-CIO board.

This indifferent attitude, which was stupidly suicidal considering the demise of labor membership, which has seen union membership decline in the past 30 years from 20.1% in 1983 to the current low of 10.5% in 2018, 14.7 million workers, almost half of what it was in 1983.

It discredits the vast majority of unions which are decent, dedicated and refute the Hollywood and TV characterization of unions as Mob dominated and corrupt. The corruption that exists in labor unions is facilitated by the ease in which criminals can misuse union funds because of the Department of Labor's (DOL), indifferent oversight and inadequate enforcement. Add to that the failure of the accounting profession to meet their professional audit and ethical standards in auditing labor unions. The watchdogs aren't watching and when they are they aren't barking. Not a damn thing changed after the Senate Hearing. The DOL probably didn't even read it.

While criminal activities exist in some labor unions, the vast majority of the country's unions are staffed by honest often dedicated people who believe in unions and treat their members with relative decency. In fact, the 20,106 private sector local unions have a better record for integrity than the 3,000,000 corporations. One study reported in the New York Times stated 11 to 13% of large companies are committing fraud. About 400 locals out of 30,000 reputed to be Mob influenced, that's about .01%

The book _Corporate Whistleblowing in 2017_ cites an anonymous survey of 500 financial service professionals in the U.S. and UK by Labaton Sucharow, a law firm, found that 40% believed their competitors engaged in illegal or unethical behavior, 24% thought you had to do it to succeed, and 16% admitted they would do it if they knew they would not be caught. The comprehensive book also states that some U.S employers, 16%, are discouraging whistleblowing with confidentiality agreements, threats of lawsuits, other retaliation, creating what they call an 'omerta culture".

James Comey our former FBI Director once in a speech to his prosecutors asked who had never had an acquittal, or a hung jury and a lot of hands shot up, he stunned them with "You are members of what we like to call the Chickenshit Club". (Related in a great book called the Chickenshit Club by Jesse Eisinger subtitle: Why the Justice Department Fails to prosecute Executives.)The last two lines in his book: "But today the United States remains unable to punish the powerful. They still have impunity."

These are facts that give the cliche "getting away with murder" a whole new meaning. The Chicago Outfit's take from organized crime is petty cash compared to organized corporate crime and its murder rate is insignificant compared to corporate killings. The Harvard Law Record Street says they estimate corporate crime to be 4.5 billion. Only 2% of corporate crimes result in imprisonment, and the very few who go to jail serve on average a mere 16 months. The street criminal goes to jail for an average of 5 years, and the conviction rate for street crime is 25% higher than white-collar crime.

It's said that street crime is different it has violence in it yet corporate criminal neglect costs tens of thousands of deaths every year. There are 14,000 murders every year but 54,000 die on the job every year or from black lung asbestos, bad food, dangerous consumer products, medical malpractice, pollution, etc. Now we have corporate contribution to and opposition to climate change, which might do us all in.

A very recent book profound in its statements and comprehensive in its findings and to me, one of the most expert ones I have read on ethics in our society relative to money and influence and the impact of whistleblowing in fighting is "Crisis of Conscience: Whistleblowing in the Age of Fraud".

It depicts in great detail with full bibliography the experiences of whistleblowers in major areas of our society such as healthcare, law, government agencies, nuclear industry, banking, and finance, academia, etc. This book is an education we all need. Tom Mueller is the author.

Despite the findings of the Senate hearings in the Eighties the government did nothing to change things, and the International continued their financial abuses, an amazing display of governmental ineptitude and/or indifference. Or more likely, blatant political motivation, fear of alienating union votes. The many financial perks honoring men whose contributions to labor have been to spend their careers demeaning its principles and exploiting its members is outrageous. This stands in stark contrast to the pensions available to men and women who do the hard, dirty, unrecognized work of washing dishes, cleaning toilets, running errands, carrying trays, cleaning hotel rooms, cooking meals and maintaining services we find critical to our comfort and well-being. The injustice burned in me. I found it impossible to accept and found it intolerable that others accepted it; It made morality a farce.

A banquet waiter retired in 2000 in San Francisco after 30 years of service, his pension....$40 a month. He only survived on the generosity of friends. My Aunt Lillian retired after 32 years of service in a hospital as a nurses' aide in Chicago in 1988 on $45 a month. These types of benefits seem relative to labor in developing countries not in the United States. The disparity between the officers' lucrative retirement benefits and the average worker could only be characterized as obscene as the differential between many corporate officers and their employees.

Greasing palms and keeping everybody happy was an intrinsic part of the philosophy of Hanley, like Jimmy Hoffa, he worked under the theory that they could buy everybody. Sharing the wealth (as long as it wasn't too much) was a tried-and-true way of keeping everyone's goodwill. The good will of the rank and file didn't matter. What they didn't know couldn't upset them. If they were lucky, they got a nickel an hour wage increase and perhaps some benefits when their contract came up every few years. If they didn't, well that was tough, blame it on the employer. After one negotiation, it reports Hanley to have said, "Let's get out of here before the members find out what we've done." Nobody knows how many employers may have bought their way out of legitimate labor contracts with the union.

I slept that night with a conflicting set of emotions: there was a sense of outrage and anger both at the Mob for financially raping the union and at the government and accounting firm for letting them get away with it. There was a growing desire to change things and the fear that I would try to do something about it. I felt myself being pulled both ways emotionally. but the need to do something was overcoming the fear. I felt the spirit of Don Quixote stirring within me once more. I thought about it for two months, weighing the risks, wondering how realistic I was being (or how unrealistic) and how it would work out.

I realized I was stepping into something that was way beyond my abilities, and the possibility to make real change not only very unlikely, it even seemed preposterous that I or anyone could, since not even the government or press had achieved it for decades. I was very aware of the physical danger involved. But what I knew, deep down from the beginning, despite the internal debate going on in myself, that I would do it. I tried to figure out how I might approach the whole thing. Who would be safe to contact? Who could I trust? Who would be most effective? I dismissed the idea of connecting with the Department of Labor. They already knew what was going on and hadn't acted on that knowledge.

I understood whistleblowing was often a thankless job and that this kind of whistleblowing could be very dangerous. "Shoot the messenger" can have a literal rather than a literary meaning with the Mob. Having worked in the government, I did not have great faith in either their ability or motivation to protect whistleblowers. The government encourages people to be "good citizens" and help law enforcement and then treats them as they're expendable. Law enforcement has little respect or regard for whistleblowers and seems to believe that their motivation is always devious. They figure they have a personal vendetta going or are looking for some money.

This is a bias not confined to the government. It's what I call the Judas bias. Judas Iscariot, the treasurer (read accountant) of the Apostles is, if one accepts the biblical account, he who blew the whistle on Jesus. They paid him thirty pieces of silver, but the money was probably incidental to his real motivation, which has been a subject of intense speculation for 2000 years. Whether it jealously, revenge, disillusionment with Jesus or just greed, the motivation of one of our earliest and history's most notorious whistleblower is still unknown. However, the rap on Judas is one that has carried forward on whistleblowers for the centuries, i.e., there has to be a sinister underlying motive to whistleblowing. I suggest we are all imprinted with the mark of the biblical whistleblower, Judas.

The union constitution required anyone with a complaint against it to use internal procedures to resolve it. Hanley had the ultimate decision on the validity of the complaint. Obviously, the complaint cards were stacked. For myself it would have been absurd to go through complaining about Mafia influence and corruption to the man who was most involved in it. I would have been whistled right out of the union. Going outside the union was the only rational thing to do.

I've often wondered how other people dealt with ethical dilemmas. What does the surgical nurse do when she knows of an incompetent or irresponsible surgeon or the mechanic who is told to find "problems" in a motorist's car or to put in inferior parts, sales people selling inferior or dangerous products, faulty building construction, or inspection, the crooked cop, lawyer, or judge? Perhaps it's the corporate attorney who knows of improper political contributions or the property manager who knows of fire code violations in his building the owner won't fix and who pays off the building inspectors.

Maybe it's the insurance salesman who knows his company cops out on legitimate claims or the payroll clerk who knows the company is guilty of wage theft. Perhaps it's the traffic court clerk who knows traffic tickets are being fixed. Larry, a guy from my neighborhood worked for the DMV in Chicago, asked me to send him people who would pay him off for passing the driving test. He considered it normal. How many accidents or even fatalities would result from those payoffs? The list of whistleblowing opportunities is endless and ubiquitous.

I believe almost everyone in their lives encounters situations where something wrong is going on. Only cloistered monks, if even they, might escape this existential challenge. One wonders why it took so long for the whistle to blow on sexual abuse in the Catholic Church when many inside and outside of the church knew of its existence for years. (I had a therapist in the Eighties tell me I was lucky not to have gone into the Seminary as a boy.) Think of the misery that could have been avoided if someone had acted years ago. In 1994 some Canadian surgical nurses tried repeatedly to call attention to the deaths of 12 babies treated by a surgeon, they determined five of them to be due to surgical error or mismanagement and preventable. Three more might have been saved if transferred to a larger hospital. One wonders how commonplace this might be.

Most people ignore those situations that do not directly impact them. And our societal emphasis on individualism encourages this kind of behavior. Our society disapproves of whistleblowing with labels such as "tattle-tale", "telling tales out of school" to" informant" to "back-stabber" to "trouble-maker" to "fink" to "snitch" which discourages whistleblowing. And minding one's own business is a time-honored approach to trouble-free survival. Some put on moral blinders saying it was none of their business or the more morally calloused say that ethics don't matter or exist. The latter groups are the ones that frighten me the most.

I decided I either had to do something about the situation or get out of the union. I had a trade as an accountant; I could find another job with relative ease. But I also had this persistent desire, even need, to do something about the injustices. I knew that most of the 330,000 members of the International were people struggling to survive, to keep their heads above the drowning waters of poverty. predominately minorities (African-Americans, legal and illegal Latinos, Asians), many uneducated, often with limited skills, and more often poor. The vast majority were inactive in the union, a large number did not know the language, and even those that understood English didn't understand their rights.

They joined the union to get a job and some protection from exploitative employers. There was a 30% turnover in union membership every year. They were a highly vulnerable, passive group and corruption flourishes in apathy. For many of these people, the next step down would be welfare if they were eligible for it. The members were paying one of the highest percentage of their dues in the labor movement to the International, money that had the special trust of brotherhood according to union tradition. But this was money that would enrich a bunch of greedy bastards who cared little about their welfare. The injustice incensed me.

I know intimately what it was like to be poor. My father, unable to cope with his alcoholism, barely supported the family when home, and after he left, never gave us a dime, nothing. If he had taken a vow never to do anything for us (which I know he didn't do) he would have kept that vow completely. In retrospect, I find this complete lack of support rather remarkable. I've never understood why my mother didn't act to force him to provide some support. It's possible she had a secret guilt for contributing to his self-destruction.

He moved around the neighborhood but stayed within walking distance of our flat (he never learned to drive) and continued to frequent the neighborhood bars. My aunt said they "had everything" when they married. Some remnants remained: a well built, still fashionable enamel coated kitchen stove and a mahogany dining room table. The rest of the furniture, like the marriage, had deteriorated. So what happened to this good start, I'll never know, but I think the relationship had much to do with it. My sister told me many years later how my father told her he had to "chase her around the table to have sex". My read on my mother was that she had little respect or interest in sex. I remember her being revolted by French kissing in movies. She lived decades without a romantic relationship after the separation (being Catholic, they never divorced).

She may have rejected a man who couldn't deal with rejection. When my father was hospitalized for heavy drinking in his sixties, they had him meet with a psychiatrist. He later told us his father had rejected him as a boy and that became the source of his problems. I remember then how his sister, my Aunt Margaret, another heavy drinker, told me the father "was a mean old bastard". It seemed like a psychological, pathological chain, his father, my father, me and if I had married and had a boy? Despite his cruel treatment of me and the gross familial neglect I always viewed him as a pathetic victim, when sober he always seemed to be searching for answers which didn't come. I think he built such a terrible train of failure he couldn't go back and face it and kept running and running from it.

One time when visiting him, he was sober and I could see he had something on his mind; He kept glancing over at me while we listened to the White Sox ballgame on the radio. I looked over at him. "Will you bury me?" he asked. I just nodded. He lived until 73, despite his hard drinking and his two packs of camels every day. Finally, his drinking and age caught up with him. He had been drinking heavily, his room in shambles, and he had not been eating. I opened a drawer, and it swarmed to the top with cockroaches. Food rotting on the stove and sinks. It smelled like hell. They admitted him to the hospital where they pumped him out and sobered him up. They said he was hallucinating.

The Chicago Transit Authority forced him to retire early. My sister arranged to have him live on a Catholic monastery in Indiana where he worked as a groundskeeper during his last years. He behaved himself as far as I know and somehow got himself an occasional bottle which the priests overlooked. I suspect he did a good job; He had been raised on Irish turf and knew how to handle the ground. I visited my father there (first time in ten years) when he became ill. The visit was perfunctory, both uncomfortable, nothing meaningful was said or happened. He knew the visit came out of duty not love and so did I. On the way back, with two priests who were driving to Chicago where they were attending the monastery funeral of a priest. They were laughing and carrying on in the front seat. It struck me as bizarre until I realized they believed he had died and gone to heaven and that was something to celebrate not mourn.

The diagnosis for my father was colon cancer. When he was dying, I sat in the room near his bed. I realized he didn't seem to be suffering, just very weak, it surprised me since I always thought cancer was a painful death. He wasn't on any medication that I knew about, but he was always tough physically; He had to be to endure the self destruction he inflicted on himself. I knew he would be dead soon. I offered him my hand and smiled at him for the first time in my life and asked, "Are we friends?" "God yes," he said, and grabbed my hand. I'm glad I did that. (He later told my brother I had smiled at him, sad stuff) I buried him afterwards, keeping my promise.

I wrote the following poem which I've recited at a poetry reading I gave. I debated whether to do it since it was so personal but curiously it was a kind of elegy to him as well. It still gets to me when I read it:

THE LAST ACT

It all seemed like a bad play, a death drama with an old plot: the absent profligate father, his alcoholic body failing at last, his legacy: empty bottles, cigarette butts, is carried in for his final appearance by six men who never knew him.

The church pews were starkly empty, except for some obligatory attendance. prayers echoed through the still air.

The priest who never met him extolled his virtues, sent him to heaven.

I thought of Hamlet's "churlish priest"

I paid him $75 for his ecclesiastical act.

The price of admission was pain.

The small audience was dutifully attentive, but showed no emotion, shed no tears.

We were there, not to mourn, but to bury our hate, our love, our father's memory.

Each had their own unhappy script.

I stayed through the last act.

The six rented pallbearers carried him out since there was not six people out of his long life that cared enough to do that for him, a mute testimony to his loveless self.

His exit, as humiliating as his life, his loneliness following him in his death.

His last act had been to rise from his deathbed, kneel on the hard wooden bedroom floor, lift his tortured face to the heavens raise his arm and shake his fist at the god who had forsaken him, who had watched his self-destructive life, and left him for dead long before he died.

He won't rest in peace, and neither shall we.

He who was never accepted alive will yield his broken body to a Nature that will accept him,

No one will really mourn, only remember.

Some years later, I visited his grave in a Chicago cemetery and told him aloud how I felt about our lives. I remembered a picture (still have it) of him sitting, dapper in a suit, hat and tie, in Lincoln park smiling, surrounded by my admiring mother and her two sisters. The man who had fought in Ireland and spent a year and a half in Dublin's Mount Joy prison (an ironic name for a prison) after his capture. He was very lucky not to have been summarily executed. They did that, at that point in the war, and his squad had assassinated a Royal Irish Constabulary. His name shows up in a book published many years later, a one liner as a member of a "flying squad". He left Ireland a patriot, then over time devolved into this hollow shell of a man, who filled his void with drink. My rant at the grave was a belated emotional expression, perhaps I hoped for some resolution, reconciliation, release. There was none, the Gestalt didn't take. I never went back.

I knew the inferiority and indifference that the poor feel, that sense of somehow not being as good as everyone else. As I passed by restaurants, I would look in and understand I would not eat in them. I knew the constant insecurity of poverty. Our rent was in arrears for months; we didn't answer the door for bill collectors, (although we always did pay our bills). We would freeze in our steps until he left the door, not talking or moving, pretending nobody was home. The flat, despite my mother's best efforts to keep it clean, had many cockroaches and an occasional rat, (my mother broke a broom one night trying to kill one). I used to watch the roaches cross the ceiling above me from my bed, afraid they would fall on my mouth. Other times I killed them with a vengeance. My sister walked out on our old back porch one day and fell through the rotting planks, fortunately catching herself with her arms.

Our food supply was often day to day and insecurity became a way of life.

We rarely made it to the next payday without a crisis for carfare, food, rent, and unpleasant expense surprises. We didn't have a bank account and went to the currency exchange to pay bills. I made and ate everything from mustard sandwiches to onion sandwiches (not bad with butter) to sugar sandwiches. If one had the ability to accept whatever one found to eat it really wasn't all that bad. I missed meals but I don't remember being really hungry that often. There always seemed to be something to eat even if it came down to taking back some coke bottles for the deposit and buying a candy bar or a Twinkie. I tried to accept poverty the way one accepts the weather, a fact of life you can't do anything about. Religion had taught me that being poor should be ennobling and at times I felt even superior to the rich. That rationalization didn't hold up to the reality of being poor but it worked for me.

My high school tuition was never paid and I remember the shame and embarrassment of being periodically called into the Dean's office about it. I would stand at the door until the dour, pock-marked Dean called me in, asked me why it wasn't paid. I would say I didn't know and he would curtly dismiss me. The ritual never got easy. My teeth had untreated cavities; My shoes often had holes, I needed glasses for years. I had an uncorrected congenital double hernia until 17. I used to wonder why it hurt to run hard. We had no car, no TV, and used a wooden window box to store food until we got an icebox. As a little boy, I promised my mother that someday I would buy her a refrigerator. She would smile sadly and pat me on the head. I don't think she believed it; she was too used to broken promises.

I remembered my mother staring out the window of our third-floor flat (a slum, a rude schoolmate had once called it). Her face was lined with anxiety as she tried to figure out how she would get through to her next payday. A scene which now reminds me of the famous Dorothea Lange Depression photo of the farm-worker mother, her face filled with that awful anxious insecurity. We had no help, no welfare, no real friends, or relatives willing to help beyond loaning a few dollars rarely. I took notes from my mother to grocery stores asking for food "until payday", my brother and sister took off when they saw the errand coming, I couldn't do that). It was hard to do, when I knew we hadn't paid the prior bill yet, but I repressed my feelings and did it with a sense of duty. I could feel the resentment of the grocer as he reluctantly put the few items in a paper bag. "Tell your mother this is the last time," he said. I know all about the shame and humiliation of poverty.

When my mother received a rare tip, we celebrated. My mother would refer to our ups and downs as "feast and famine days". (The horrible Irish famine wherein one million Irish men, women, and children died of starvation) is deep in the minds of the Irish although they never spoke of it back then, they did their best to repress it. I visited the Famine Museum in Roscommon County, where my parents immigrated from and saw the somber monuments to it in Dublin. The Quakers did some of the most effective relief work, (I sent them a $500 contribution, telling them, "I owe you." The English, had a dark view of the Irish as ignorant louts who did nothing, but screw and eat potatoes provided reluctant and inadequate aid. They had a Malthusian view of the Irish, let Nature (i.e., starvation) reduce their excessive numbers.

The view of the government it was an "Act of God" to reform and rejuvenate the Irish people. They had a kind of laissez-faire attitude which doomed so many of the Irish population to starvation. I still don't understand how my ancestors survived, they owned land which was critical but how did they keep others from eating their crops? I asked about this but was ignored. I have to wonder whether there is something shameful in their history they rather not address.

I felt comfortable in Ireland like I belonged there. I was embedded with some Irish Nationalism from the ballads my mother used to sing to us as we all looked out on Clark Street on a Sunday evening. I visited the prison in Dublin (now a museum) where my uncle did time. The most unforgiving place I've ever been in: Small, dank, dark cells with window slots for light, hard rock walls. Kilmainham Gaol, also the place where they executed the Irish rebels of the 1916 Easter Rising. It was the beginning of the Irish struggle for independence led by a fascinating group of poets, actors, writers, teachers, and one former military men. They knew their rebellion was doomed and would lead to their deaths, it was called "the failure that succeeded".

Somehow, my ancestors survived their famine and somehow we survived ours. My mother had a wonderful sense of gallows humor that I admired for its tenacious courage and its humor. Hers was a hard, lonely, depressed kind of life that only a strong sense of duty and a dedication to save her family seemed to sustain. Interestingly, my mother, who was a housekeeper in downtown hotels, was a member of HEREIU. "That old union" she used to say, "they do nothing for us". She worked as a domestic when she came to the country from Ireland at 17 and like many Irish women of the time knew no other work than this kind of service.

At the union, I thought of housekeepers employed for a paltry minimum wage in hotels, working like slaves to clean up a room every half hour of the workday. It is one of the more revealing anomalies of our culture that housekeepers are rarely tipped. Customers will readily tip a waitress for calling in an order and walking 20 feet to a table to deliver it. They will slip a tip to a bartender for taking 30 seconds to pour a drink in a shot glass. But most are oblivious to any need to tip a maid who has spent 30 to 60 minutes cleaning up their toilet, making their bed, vacuuming their rug and doing all the things that make a room comfortable. (Maybe we tip only when we have to, when there is someone watching, when there is a threat of being considered "cheap" or when we get a smile and thank you as a reward.)

It's difficult for me to explain or express the passion I felt for the people in the union. I've always been known for not displaying emotion. "The Coolest son- of-a-bitch I ever saw" was one comment about me from a guy I knew when involved in a tense desegregation effort at a company I worked for, Sinclair Oil, who still practiced segregation in a Chicago downtown billing office in the late Sixties. I was friendly to blacks in my barracks in the Army so doing the same in the Seventies in Chicago seemed normal to me but not with the two managers from Atlanta and some white clerks.

Despite the pressure, which approached violence, I continued having lunch and breaks with the black guys. I changed nothing, but I held my own and made the point. I seemed the only one who wasn't very emotional about the whole affair. My sister-in-law used to ask me how I "mastered my feelings". It wasn't so much a question of mastery or even courage but the ability to shut down feelings and fear. But the emotion I felt for the poor was and is very present and profoundly deep. I still go to protests and was arrested in 2013 as part of the poor people's Moral Monday movement. (First time I was arrested for a *good* cause).

I can't remember crying more than a handful of times in my life but when I thought about the plight and poverty of the members tears would almost come to my eyes. I don't know how much of that deep empathy was for them or myself perhaps both, but it was a very powerful motivation. I formed a bond with the members, a bond of mutually shared poverty and pain more powerful than any relationship I have ever had. There was nothing, absolutely nothing, I wouldn't do to change things.

In October I contacted the government to try to do something about it. I knew it was unrealistic to think I, an individual with almost no power, could affect this change but I also knew I was in a unique position to do something because of being inside the union. I thought about the time it would take; I thought about getting caught; I rationalized my decision by telling myself something that I never did believe, that I would merely collect some incriminating information, give it to the government and go on my way.

I picked out the name of a staff attorney from the Senate report, Steve Ryan, and called him up. He was at first surprised, then interested, and cautionary, "Don't keep obvious notes, use a code" he said and then "You don't have to do this, you know". "I know," I said, but I did have to do it. Ryan asked me to call him back in a week. He would arrange a meeting with the Chief of the Organized Crime Task-force in Chicago, a man named Mike Anderson. We met in the attorney's Chevy Chase apartment. Mike Anderson, a gray-haired, distinguished looking man sat in a chair smiling. The attorney's wife looked pale and nervous and so did he. We went to dinner at a neighborhood diner, leaving the worried wife in the apartment. The attorney, a stocky man in his late thirties or early forties, ordered a drink and quickly downed it looking around the restaurant nervously. I realized he was concerned he was being set up since he had acted as an interrogator during the Subcommittee investigations. He relaxed when I told him I once worked for the IRS and had no criminal record.

Anderson and I talked. "We must run a criminal check on you before we do anything else." I nodded, "no problem". He said they had little or almost no information on the International. I told him I would help change that and I said, (although I felt somewhat silly doing it), "I want to be referred to as Robert Holt whenever you or your agents talk about me outside the office". I didn't want my name bandied about especially in bars and restaurants where it might get back to the union. I got the name from a curious short story I had read years before about this fictitious guy Robert Holt, who is a nondescript character, a characteristic perhaps I hoped to duplicate in this role, (after all Don Quixote was not the Don's real name). Anderson was humoring me when he said, "Okay, we'll call you Robert Holt."

We shook hands, and I left. I was now an official whistleblower.

I didn't know much about whistleblowing protection laws at the time I was making my decision but smart enough to know that organizations invariably retaliated and that retaliation was very hard to prove. My later research confirmed that insight in spades. Despite passage of the Civil Service Reform Act (CSRA) in 1978, the first legislation protecting whistleblowers and the important Whistleblower protection Act (WPA) reinforced in 1989 along with the Sarbanes Oxley 2002 regulations, whistleblowers have had limited success in tying retaliation to their whistleblowing activities.

It's notable that that despite the collaborate system of corporate complicity in the cause of the 2008 sub-prime and derivative fraud that led to the "Great Recession" no Racketeering Influenced and Corrupt Organizations (RICO) lawsuit was ever filed. The practicing Law Institute's "Corporate Whistleblowing in 2017" concludes that "Without an aggressive plan to stamp out misconduct we are waiting for another financial disaster to strike". Place your bets now.

Dodd Frank legislation provides rewards for SEC whistleblowers for up to 10% to 30% of any monetary recovery over 1 million dollars. According to the SEC, they established the program in August 2011. As of 2018, the SEC has paid out 326 million resulting in a return of 1.7 billion to the U.S. Treasury. There were over 5200 whistleblowing tips in 2018, which resulted in a 168 million payout to 13 individuals in 2018. Not bad, if I were a young accountant, I would be tempted to learn forensic accounting and go hunting in certain industries.

But these awards to a few dozen whistleblowers are excessive and haven't helped many other whistleblowers who have sacrificed financially, just a few high profile ones. I would like to see the money spread around rather than like huge lottery prizes only given to a few. For every person who winds up a hero in the public eye in a movie or get a cash reward, there are hundreds who pay the exorbitant psychological, physical and financial price of whistleblowing and get little or no recognition or reward.

Here is a link to an interesting article and study by two researchers entitled "Whistling Blowing Doesn't Work." I disagree with their conclusions, but there are some good points and it gives the other side of the phenomena of whistleblowing. It's on the Skeptic magazine's website, scroll down to the piece on https://www.skeptic.com/eskeptic/14-08-06/

CHAPTER FIVE:
I GO SHOPPING

One of the biggest lies in the world is that crime doesn't pay,
of course, crime pays
- G. Gordon Liddy

I began feeding Anderson general information on the union, some of it very basic, such as rosters of the union locals, newsletters, phone directories of personnel, financials, all background stuff. Ryan reaffirmed that the Feds had almost no information on the union. I learned that Hanley was a "national target" and the government had been "after" Hanley since he took over the union in 1973 but had never got him. The Feds had called his presidency "a classic take-over of a union by organized crime." Hanley aggressively set about changing the union's by-laws to merge welfare funds, consolidate locals, invest in real estate and make political contributions through a member supported political action committee called T.I.P. (To Insure Progress).

One outrageous change was a clause authorizing payment of legal expenses for union members. While on the surface this seems reasonable if the members are not at fault in the line of duty but the clause could be interpreted broadly enough to include just about any legal defense fees including criminal activity. Hanley was setting up some insurance for himself and the boys. Legal fees for John Gibson who despite being convicted of embezzling union funds, came in over $300,000 and paid by the union under this authorization. Other convicted embezzlers at the local level had their legal fees paid by the union, compounding their financial damage on their members.

The victims pay the legal fees of the perpetrators for their fraud against them. This one bothered me a lot. I also learned that the government had been investigating some large local welfare funds that were suffering large losses through insurance fraud and malfeasance. One scam involved doctors in health care plans that received the union business and then gave kickbacks. They were also manipulating the number of cases they worked to increase the amount they got from the welfare funds. I was able to access the financial records of the funds at the CPA firm and spent several nights going through them.

I developed some statistics that did show the administrator failing to oversee the funds properly, facts which somehow seemed to elude the Havey accountants. I sent it on to Anderson who was impressed but I then learned that the DOL settled their lawsuit with the administrator. "Settling" financial fraud rather than preventing or prosecuting it seems to be the government's preference in these cases, the easy way out and not one that deters future corruption.

My experience with and in government has always led me to believe that they believed first in rules and regulations and people second. In dealing with the Organized Crime Task Force I drafted a letter, through a public interest attorney I contacted, to the government telling them of my intention to help them, showing I wanted no compensation, and declining any immunity from prosecution. I wanted to establish two things: one a relationship of trust and two, proof that I had a relationship with the government. I did not want them to disown me if I got in legal trouble for my activities. In fact, I asked if they would help in that regard (although I doubted that they would).

A few weeks later the attorney received a letter from the government's attorney acknowledging mine, telling me that while they "deeply appreciated my efforts": They could not offer any help on any legal problems that might develop nor guarantee any protection beyond the Witness Protection Program. The response didn't surprise me; working with the government is a one-way street with them in the driver's seat and you as an uninsured passenger. I still have that letter. But I established I had a relationship with them.

Hanley's dominance over the union was complete. One week, I spent long nights going through over a thousand financial "propositions" covering a five-year period, (expenditures over $2000 which had to be approved by the executive board members). I was interested in knowing not only what the money was for but also whether there was any discussion, debate, or objections by the General Executive Board. Although I shouldn't have been, I was still somewhat shocked when I found no negative votes and only one real abstention in all the hundreds of propositions I looked at that week.

One female VP had reservations about a $14,000 legal bill for Hanley's Fifth Amendment silence during the Senate hearings but she signed off on it after pressure.)It showed, a rubber-stamp executive board. Whatever Hanley wanted Hanley got, and no one had the guts or enough concern to protest any expenditure no matter how outrageous. They approved many of the propositions after the fact, after Hanley had done whatever he wanted to do.

What I saw that week was the dues money of the members flowing out of the union like "monopoly" money. Huge salary increases for favorite employees (including 10% annual increases for officers); unlimited expense accounts for them and other favorite officials (I saw one monthly expense account for $30,000 by a general officer on a European junket); leased luxury automobile; per diem travel payments to officials who rarely traveled and who were reimbursed through expense accounts when they did, creating a "double dip" on travel expenses,(per diem is a fixed amount paid to a person on the road to cover expenses); the International did an interesting twist on this item by paying officers $100 a day, ($36,500 a year) whether-or-not they traveled. Not a bad perk.

Hanley told Senate investigators that it was "tip money". I checked that comment and found that his expense account listed his tips even ones without receipts so he was being reimbursed for the tips and pocketing the per diem money. The "tip money" became all gravy. Later, in a final burst of creative greed, they converted all the per diem payments (over a half million dollars) to permanent salary increases. Twenty- six vice-presidents existed on the payroll (making a local officer a Vice president became a sure way to lock him or her into Hanley's loyal cadre). They paid administrative aides a bonus $2000 just to attend the general convention and $2000-$4000 for attending executive board meetings.

These "gratuities" to employees further bought loyalty. Employees seemed just as casual about expenses spending over a million dollars in Federal Express charges alone in 5 years, costs were just never considered much in the union's activities.

Ironically, the HEREIU constitution states that "Union funds are to be held in sacred trust for the benefit of the membership". And the benefits adhered to the officers, not the members. All the health and death benefits that could have been given didn't happen. Nor were workplace and safety conditions, stronger job security, better pay, and pensions, a reduction in the high dues, and more effective organizing and collective bargaining by the union. They screwed them out of all these benefits by their wanton spending of International funds.

I'm a library buff and I like research. My idea of an interesting time isn't going to the movies or to a ballgame but filtering through card catalogs (this pre-Internet time) to find books that have that piece of information I want. I began to spend hours in law libraries reading about the laws and regulations governing labor unions. I looked up cases brought by the government against labor unions. I read about the fiduciary obligations of union officers. I would stay until late at night, often closing the library taking notes or making copies of citations on case law. I seemed to be the only person who thought they were breaking labor laws or the only one taking it seriously.

When on the road, I kept my expenses down whenever I could, avoiding first-class hotels. I had the reputation of being "frugal" and Leavitt expressed his annoyance with me one time when I didn't want to stay at the plush Beverly Hills Hilton, "stay there" he commanded, I did. However, I always disliked first class. I don't appreciate patronizing service; I don't need someone to tuck me in at night; I don't need a chocolate on my pillow (although I'll eat it if it's there). I can open my own doors and even carry my own baggage. While I can appreciate appropriate help and an occasional luxury, paying an exorbitant amount for a room or a dinner has always made me uncomfortable. It seems to me like such a damn waste. And I thought we should treat the member's money with more respect. Why should we live in luxury off their money; most of them sure as hell weren't living in luxury.

I worked briefly at his office, I forget why but I wanted to scout it but he had put the secretary on to keep up on my movements. I caught that right away, she wasn't too subtle. She left at five and I went through some files, but Leavitt's desk was locked as was the file in his office. Next day she asked me how long I stayed. I told her I left shortly after her and went to a movie, I named it because I somehow had seen it playing in the paper. She nodded and that seemed to satisfy her. She obviously knew of the movie.

There were over $300,000 in propositions for building a restaurant and bar on the upper floor of the International headquarters. The plush bar was a replica of a famous San Francisco bar. Most of the International's general officers liked to drink (it almost seemed like a prerequisite for the job), and they liked to drink in style. They liked to live in style too and their expense accounts reflected that fact. There were stretch limousines for officers, a chauffeur for Hanley, a luxury condo in D.C., two pilots and a part-time attendant for the Sabre jet, extravagant charitable contributions heavily biased toward Irish and Catholic related charities. ($250,000 to renovate old St. Patrick's church in Chicago, for example, while an African-American activist church in D.C. received $1000).

There were many contributions to golfing events (Hanley liked to golf), and even $2000 for dog sled races (union dogs no doubt). Hanley's extravagant (too mild a word, let's say extraordinary) contributions to Irish sporting groups, ($450,000 to the Irish-American Sports Federation alone), led to a basketball stadium being named after him in Ireland. He brought over 34 relatives and friends to Ireland for the event, all expenses paid by the union. I searched but I couldn't find that stadium in Ireland today. (Too bad Ed)

While some charities were worthy, they had little or nothing to do with labor and done in a self-aggrandizing manner by the president and reflected his personal preferences and ego not the membership's interests. Ironically, Hanley in his personal life was anything but philanthropic with his own money. His tax returns for some years showed absolutely nothing in charitable contributions except for a horse (likely too old to ride, to a non-profit). Most labor union charitable contributions have some labor-related element in them. They made big contributions to the Irish Catholic world. Beyond the general officers, Irish Catholics were a distinct minority in a membership made up of African-Americans, Latinos, Asians, and many protestant Americans so that many of the contributions sure as hell didn't reflect their charitable interests. And the organization was, after all, a union not a private charitable foundation.

I found a cadre of "consultants" receiving tens of thousands of dollars a month. Some names were familiar, like Pat Marcy, a committeeman in the notorious First Ward in Chicago for many years and whose son Pat Marcy Jr. received $213,700 over eight years for "public relations work." Several other consultants and attorneys received similar amounts over long periods of time. There was no written record of services for most of those fees or those of most of the "consultants". Some consultants claimed they provided "oral reports" to Hanley. I'd love to hear some of those ghost consulting conversations.

For some, the payments went on for years amounting to hundreds of thousands of dollars. Some received leased cars and auto insurance. I learned later Hanley's wife drove a $63,000 Cadillac courtesy of the International. Paul Burke, a onetime TV actor and neighbor of Hanley received $25,000 a year, and a leased car for providing a "celebrity presence" at HEREIU affairs. Legal and accounting fees almost prohibitive. Jack Reynolds, a Chicago attorney, received a million and a half dollars for legal work between 1986 and 1991.

Administratively, the International was in chaos. Per capita dues from many of the locals were seriously in arrears (some of them knowing what the International was doing with their money did everything they could to avoid payment). At one point, I found a statement that showed delinquent per capita dues totaling 16 million dollars. The International didn't worry about it, when they needed money they raised the per capita tax and collected it from those locals who, out of duty or fear, paid their dues faithfully. They had their proverbial "cash cow" that could be milked anytime they wanted more financial nourishment.

Hanley was especially generous to politicians and certain politicians. In one 18-month period he gave a half million dollars to them. He played golf with the late Tip O'Neill, former speaker of the House and contributed to his campaigns. Hanley sent George Ryan the previous Governor of Illinois $50,000. Asked by a journalist if the Governor had any reservations about accepting the money his press man spun the situation by saying "no", because the union members had endorsed the Governor, "What the officers of the union do doesn't reflect on the members," he said. The Governor understood that the members had no voice in who the union leadership endorsed, who got the money or how much but it was their money. Ryan later spent five years in prison for corruption, a denouement that too many Illinois governors have had. It became almost like a career stop for them.

Neither the DOL nor CPA firm questioned these expenditures. Politicians weren't looking for votes from the union, the members comprised no voting block, many weren't eligible and many didn't bother. Politicos only looked for contributions and they got them through the union's T.I.P. (To Insure Progress) PAC fund which doled out money to them. The T.I.P. fund funded by the members who had no voice on how it was spent.

Eugene H. Methvin, a former writer for the Reader's Digest, was almost a lone voice among journalists writing on corruption in unions. He later served on the 1984 president's Commission on Organized Crime. In the April 1996 issue of Reader's Digest he wrote of the close relationship between former president Clinton and his wife with Arthur Coia of the once Mob dominated Laborers International Union. The relationship included personal gifts by Coia, visits to the White House and a speech by Hilary to the Laborer's convention. Hillary Clinton spoke at a Laborers Union convention despite reservations of her advisers. (Surprised this didn't come out from the Trump people during the campaign, part of the "Hilary is a crook campaign".) The relationship of Nixon and the Teamster's Union has also been well documented. They say Nixon pardoned Jimmy Hoffa as part of a deal for Teamster support in his reelection. Our presidents have been more interested in the cash of their political supporters than their character.

Methvin was a brave man. The Mob didn't take kindly to news exposure. In 1956, Victor Riesel, who specialized in labor unions and read in 356 newspapers, was blinded by acid thrown into this face by a gangster. He was an aggressive opponent of union corruption and Mob activity, testifying before Congress and taking on the hierarchy of the Mob like Anthony Anastasio. He ignored many death threats. The acid attack occurred on a New York Street and he was blinded and it also damaged portions of his face. His attack led to widespread outrage at every level and resulted in the convictions of some Mob figures and to legislation and action to investigate Mob infiltration and influence in unions. Riesel continued to report and write. His actions afterwards, not so praiseworthy: wanting to purge homosexuals from civil service, a staunch supporter of the Hollywood Blacklist, a critic of Malcom X and espousing preventive nuclear war against China and Russia.

I have this curious mixture of skepticism and naivete in my personality. I challenge many things intellectually, but emotionally always maintain the hope that there is decency and goodness in politics. I always find it hard to believe that many politicians can be bought, intimidated, compromised, etc; I mean, don't they have a conscience; Don't they *know* what they're doing, don't they have a sense of integrity? Idealism can be a curse since one is always searching for that ideal in themselves, in people and politicians. But when one reads of how the Mob has helped presidents get elected, have dominated mayors (and even shot them), and how it spreads its money around political circles then one is jolted into realism and/or cynicism.

The reality being that the Mob has played a significant role in the political history of our country, including Joe Kennedy's relationship with the Outfit in getting his son, Jack Kennedy, elected president in 1960. According to some sources, 100,000 votes were stolen in Cook County, enough to swing Illinois to Kennedy by the barest of margins. 2%. Whether the Mob killed Kennedy because of his administration's crackdown on organized crime (through his brother Robert, as Attorney General) as some high-placed officials think is still a matter of speculation. No doubt it will be a subject of continued interest and debate for years to come. My view is that they did not.

I left the union Friday morning of that week at dawn and went to a 24-hour coffee shop on Wisconsin Avenue. My mind was swimming with numbers. I felt as if I had been reading a fiction story. I could not believe the systematic looting of the union the records revealed, and I could not believe people were letting this happen. The president, because of his position, had a legal mechanism to spend money and his dominance of the compliant general executive board allowed him to do anything he wanted with the members dues with no opposition. It was also clear that the Mafia mystique which surrounded him and the union provided him with a powerful undercurrent of intimidation which didn't even have to be expressed to enhance his domination of the union.

The members weren't privy to the financial affairs of the union. Although the DOL requested financial statements to members, the International ignored the requirement until the DOL audit picked it up. To comply they sent out a laundry list of expenses presented in such a manner as to make them meaningless. A member would have to classify all the expenses, then add them up and he/she would still not have a real picture of the financial situation of the International. The DOL did nothing more to improve the reporting situation. The DOL receives it authority to oversee unions from the Labor Management Reporting and Disclosure Act, (LMDRA) Congress passed in 1959. One wonders if they ever read it.

As I drank my coffee and reviewed the propositions I had copied, I felt a sense of impotent outrage. I knew that many of the officials and employees of the union *knew* of these expenditures. While they may have not made the studied effort, I was making they still *knew* the members were being exploited. And the Department of Labor through its periodic audits of the International *knew* it. The CPA firm performed annual certified audits and had a constant presence at the International and some of its locals so they *knew* it. They would have to be incompetent not to know it. They were intimately involved in the union's financial affairs. The lack of internal controls violated every accounting audit standard (Hanley, one consultant laconically observed "believed in a lack of structure").

DOL's Labor Racketeering Section had 61 indictments, which resulted in 38 convictions in 1986. The latest statistics from April 2018 thru March 2019 show that they did 236 audits, which resulted in 79 convictions. The box score has improved somewhat for the past 20 years both in quantity and quality, however the DOL only audits unions where there is an anomaly in their annual reports. They give "tips" on how unions can audit themselves. They do not require outside certified audits. So any union clever enough to file respectable looking reports are home free.

However, there were 15 audits of Unite-Here locals in 2015, mostly large ones, including Local One in Chicago and two big NYC locals. I looked at the financials and salaries and I have to admit on the surface things are looking good at these locals. However, I believe outside audits on unions with revenues over a certain amount are essential, we require these of many corporations. The DOL, like most government agencies, does not have the manpower or resources to cover their wide union territory of 20,000 unions.

What struck me during my days at the International was the element of unreality that existed. On the surface things seemed normal, the busy office, the typical employees, all the ordinary organizational functions: phones, computers, repairmen, sales people, paperwork coming in and going out, visitors, etc. people laughing, talking about the weather or sports and other happenings in their lives; the officers looking important, holding meetings, making plans but beneath it all, under all this seemingly normal activity, there was this *thing*. This grotesque truth, this terrible corruption taking place. The organization existed, in a way, as nothing more than a huge theatrical set with staged business and actors but with characters backstage who were playing roles quite different from the ones visible to the audience. These characters do the show looking for money not applause in their decadent drama.

One day, alone with Leavitt in his office going over the computerization schedule trying to decide which locals to do next. I started pointing out the huge programming fees billed us from the accountants, "This is too much Herman", (I meant it literally and figuratively). Leavitt shrugged his shoulders fatalistically."We're married to them," he said. He looked at me to see if I understood. I said nothing. "We're married to them," he repeated. I interpreted that comment as meaning the accountants were in bed with the union and a divorce out of the question.

I fought the accounting firm on the programming fees. They were enormous, and the program full of bugs creating serious problems at the locals. I forced a meeting between Herman, myself, and the MAS partner. I am perceptive; I know people's limitations and I know how to play those well. I knew Herman didn't like conflict, for him it might have been an age or health related aversion, at one time reputed to be pretty tough, (an earlier photo show a dark-looking man with a sly smile) and the MAS partner couldn't challenge me too aggressively since I was running the computer show and I was essentially a client.

He didn't say a word to me but addressed his comments to Herman, who sat, non-committal, listening to us and hoping the whole affair would end quickly. As I write this Herman may still be alive I saw a Herman Leavitt in Los Angeles and didn't see him on the Social Security Death Index a while back, He would be around 99. I suspect if that is so Herman wouldn't even remember me but I remember him all too well.

I won a $120,000 reduction in their fees, an event that alienated them from me. I later found they sold the program, which we had paid hundreds of thousands of dollars to develop, to another union violating our copyright. I raised the issue, but Herman didn't seem to care about it. He thought I had a temper. "You have a short fuse," he said to me one time after I had a heated discussion with another local officer. I remember him warning one officer to be careful with me before we had a meeting with him.

In fact, I never viewed myself as temperamental or tough, on the contrary, I always felt I had to struggle for the courage to do things; My early experience had left me sensitive and vulnerable in interactions. I had courage on causes and issues but not so much on personal interactions (although I've improved on that). But a sense of self-righteousness emboldened me over the wrongs in the union and I cultivated a strong image so I could deal with my adversaries in the union. The accountants were now in that group. I hated how they neglected the membership; they weren't even considering their rights as members, and they hated me for cutting into their fees.

But an important question arises. What is the public accountant's duty to the client and what is his/her duty to the public? Public accountants have a more complex and difficult tune to play as whistleblowers. While they do not have the same straight forward and rigid requirement of confidentiality that lawyers and doctors have to their clients, they have serious constraints. They have a dual loyalty with inherent ethical dilemmas since they are perceived to serve reliant third parties of their work (shareholders, creditors, members, regulators, public, etc). and their client who pays their fee and can hire or fire them at will. (I'm of the opinion independence from anyone who is paying you is damn near impossible).

The restrictions take on legal and professional aspects: legal in that in many states it is a crime for them to reveal proprietary data without client permission and professional in that the AICPA Ethics (Rule 301) consider such an act as a violation of professionalism and penalties can cause loss of their CPA license. The profession has strongly opposed and discouraged the whistleblowing outside of the "loop" (the "loop" being the internal organizational whistle). Whistleblowing auditors can lose their job and the firm's client (making their future employment more precarious). Conversely (or perversely) the auditor who does not go public is also vulnerable to lawsuits and professional sanctions, (witness the Enron Affair and the dissolution of the Arthur Anderson accounting firm, one of the world's largest.). The auditor again could lose the license to practice. Walking this ethical high wire can create dizzying dilemmas for the auditor.

The auditors at the International not only didn't follow an ethical protocol they abetted the unethical behavior of the union. I have a greater contempt for the professionals, the accountants, and lawyers who protect and give credibility to corporate and union crooks than the crooks themselves. They were criminals, and they knew it. The professionals pretended to themselves and others they were not. Much of this corruption could not exist without these professionals who prostitute themselves and their profession by collaborating with corruption. It is my view that the public interest not private interest should be the ethical standard of professionals dealing with client corruption.

The International like many organizations had an audit committee, drawn from the members, whose function ostensibly was to provide oversight of the finances of the union to protect the membership. The Secretary-Treasurer selected the audit committee for the union, who met once a year, typically had little, if any accounting background. The accountants gave them a brief presentation by the firm's managing partner, wined and dined them and they returned home. I asked one local officer who had been on the audit committee one year what he did. He laughed and winked at me, "We looked at some papers, they took us out to lunch, listened to the accountant give a talk, he showed us some bonds, and then went to dinner". Each following year, they selected a new audit committee and similarly wined and dined. They went to a party, not an audit.

I flew into Chicago to meet with the programmer at Havey's La Salle Street office. They were up on the 39th floor with a stunning panoramic view of Chicago's Loop and lakefront. I could see sailboats out on the deep blue lake and cars moving along Lake Shore Drive in a long, seemingly endless procession. During the day, I attended meetings and worked with the programmer and the head of the Havey MAS. I didn't like the guy; He screwed us on the accounting program and he didn't like me because I called him on it. At one point he left me along in his office (always a mistake for anyone to do at this point in my covert career); I probed into his laptop and then into the Havey system, but suddenly I was popped off. Someone had seen me in the office on the laptop and notified the computer operator. No one said anything since I was still the client.

Toward the end of the day, I was going through the International's work papers when I realized the staff were leaving and it was five o'clock. I hung around and continued to check out the work papers. I closed the door to the office I was in. As night fell, the remaining employees left, and I was alone in the large office. Audit work paper folders can be large bulky affairs stuffed with worksheets, documents, letters, and notes of all kinds and I patiently went through each file, each folder year by year. I didn't know what I was looking for, just *something*.

Around eight I went into the men's room and halfway back to the office I heard someone come in. I ducked into a cubicle. Whoever came in entered the cubicle right next to mine but on the opposite side. He worked there an hour while I sat motionless, breathing quietly in the next cubicle. I kept thinking, "When is this son-of-a-bitch going to leave" it felt like forever. Finally, the person left. I went back into the office and continued to survey the work papers. The janitors came in and left without noticing me. At two in the morning, I took a short break and looked out the window. I could see the light of the Marina City towers and I remembered that's where the owner of the firm, Thomas Havey lived. If I could see his lights, he could see mine. He might even see a dark figure moving around digging into file drawers. I called it a night, switched off the light and left.

I was a little nervous going downstairs wondering if the guard might be suspicious because of the time and check out my briefcase. I stopped at the mail center at the ground floor and thought about dropping the copies in a fed-x envelope, addressing them to myself and putting the envelope in the Fed-X mail drop. But I didn't have the union's account number, so I had to take the chance. I put on a weary business man's demeanor and walked to the desk in the middle of the lobby. The man at the guard station said nothing as I signed out putting in the wrong name and suite number. I had no idea of what kind of business I was supposed to be coming from and signing in for. He didn't even look at the sheet. We exchanged "good nights" and I left the building.

The International was Havey's largest account; the fees incurred by the union were almost prohibitive. They billed the union's welfare funds so relentlessly that the DOL found it necessary to place a cap on professional fees including the accounting firm. Funds suffered tremendous losses because of fraud and administrative neglect. The Senate Hearing had told of how Locals 6 and 100 of New York City reduced pension and welfare contributions for restaurant owners who paid them off. I found that huge amounts of these contributions, over 10 million dollars in 1990, were delinquent and I believe some of them were deliberately delinquent because of payoffs. I provided a list of the delinquencies to the DOL. The DOL intervened via a civil lawsuit to prevent further dilution of assets and to implement some basic business procedures in the funds.

International officials lacking even basic business skills relied to an extraordinary extent on Havey, (whom I believe cultivated the dependency), which led to extraordinary fees. The Havey firm had a revenue of 32 million dollars in 1998 and had 37 partners with 208 staff. Havey also did the accounting for several of the International's big city locals, including Local 1 in Chicago's notorious First Ward. They had a goldmine client in the International and its local unions that they could mine for endless billable hours. The proverbial cash cow.

A government investigation of Local 1 found it in financial chaos with its president, Tom Hanley, presiding over an organization verging on bankruptcy despite financial assistance of over two-and-a-half million dollars from his father thru the International. Although the union was running deficits and in deep financial difficulty, Tom Hanley continued annual salary increases for the officers. Double dipping with International Vice-presidents drawing an officer's salary from both their local and the International was commonplace but taking greed to a new level of creative opportunism Tom Hanley paid his father Ed Hanley $31,000 a year for "advice on running a union". It would be fascinating to know what kind of advice might have been, if any. These "advice" payments went on for over ten years. If there was any, it was bad advice, given the terrible results.

Even as Local 1's pension plan payments became delinquent the large annual increases to its officers continued, a scenario which would have been comic, except for its implications for the membership, occurred when the local could not produce financial statements and referred investigators to the accounting firm for financial information. The accountants confounded the investigators by telling them that the only financial information they had were "compilations" from 1990 to 1996 which were *based on the representations made by Local 1 officials. The auditors accepted this farce.* Tom Hanley, who later was appointed as Director of Organizing at the International by his father, was criticized for spending only two days a month at his D.C. office. But he was just following in the footsteps of his father who averaged about the same (25 days per year) at his International office for many years. Hanley's other son, Edward Jr. was an attorney for a firm that did business for the union. Hanley took good care of his boys.

In January 1986, Ed Hanley was arrested in a Palm Springs airport while running his carry on luggage through an x-ray device which revealed a stolen 22 caliber pistol. He was released on a $2500 bond. His explanation was classic and has to rank as one of the least creative excuses of all time: Hanley maintained his wife had "inadvertently packed the pistol in with my lunch", (a rather unusual culinary combination). How a wife "inadvertently" puts a loaded pistol in a lunch bag raises questions so existential they boggle the mind. Could it have been she suggesting something to him if he didn't like the sandwich?

Why was the $347,000 a year president with an unlimited expense account, brown-bagging it on an airplane trip where food was likely served? My guess is that Hanley must have been drinking and forgot about having the weapon on him or he was using the lunch as a cover for it. The pistol then traced to a 1974 burglary in Skoke, Illinois. Hanley received a slap on the wrist from the court and on his way. I told the DOL agent about the arrest. "What was he afraid of" the agent asked me. I didn't know, but something or someone.

I was traveling again spending a good deal of time in California locals buying computer equipment and installing the accounting program. I felt okay with working with the locals on the project since the International was paying the bill for equipment, software, and labor. It was a good deal for the locals. It also gave me the opportunity to check out the locals, and I did so methodically. I was interested in Palm Springs which was the winter vacation home of some Chicago types like Arcardo, Hanley, Grogan, and other International officials also had homes there. A petite, pretty woman who was a member of the International's welfare fund trustees and had a close personal relationship with Hanley ran the local. She was paranoid about government agents and told me, "I think they rented the office next door". I checked with Anderson, "We don't have anything there," he said.

While I was there, I met a business agent pat "the Torch" Baptista. I don't know how he earned that colorful nickname, but one could speculate. All he seemed to do as far as work was concerned when I was there was to come in around ten o'clock, make a phone call and go play golf. He had the low life foul mouth of most of these guys. Another habituate of the local was "Pinky" Schiftman, a gnome like little man with bad grammar and equally bad taste in clothes. They literally bombed him out of Miami by a car bomb and transferred to a safer assignment. I found nothing in Palm Springs and just made the female secretary-treasurer more paranoid with my late night searches in the local. She refused to let me back in the local after that trip.

I visited Vegas to talk with the two locals there about the computer program but the big Local 225 had their own computer system and was not interested in the International's version. There was also considerable tension between the Secretary-Treasurer and Hanley, an interesting situation since a prior Secretary-Treasurer, Al Bramlett, was murdered and buried in the desert. This happened, according to the testimony of Joseph

Hauser, the informant at the Senate hearing, after Blackie Leavitt had warned Bramlett, "he would wind up six feet buried in the desert."

Leavitt denied the accusation (he testified under oath at the Subcommittee hearing) and later called Hauser a "pathological liar". Bramlett had resisted turning his welfare funds over to the International but after his murder they were turned over to the HEREIU. Curiously, a father and a son named Hanley were convicted of murdering Bramlett. There was no genetic relationship between Edward Hanley and the two guys who did it were professional killers. There was speculation that the International might have had something to do with the killings but there other motivations by other parties as well. I believe Leavitt, he wouldn't have testified under oath if he was lying, he could have taken the Fifth. Looks like Hauser was the liar. As usual, nothing came out of the hearing.

I visited the Bartenders local in Vegas. This local, curiously separate from the big Vegas local, had a guy from Boston who ran it. He seemed to be a friend of Hanley. My visit was only for an hour, but I had time to find two guns in drawers and to see, for the first time in my life, a two-way mirror making the local a little like a Hollywood film set for a Mob movie. The guy from Boston bought me lunch at a casino and told me about an easy drive to Zion National park and Bryce Canyon that I could do over the weekend. So I did it and enjoyed it, a nice break from the tension. I could do this many times out west enjoying some spectacular scenery and wilderness. To avoid the monotony of motels and patronizing hotels, I bought a tent and whenever I could, I would camp out. I would stick it in the rental's trunk car and search for a state campground. Finding one I would pitch the tent and slip in my sleeping bag. It worked out well. I camped often in nice outdoor settings.

I also had taken up swimming (after being told at a health fair I was "out of shape") and became very faithful in getting into a pool three or four times a week for a half hour swim. I started watching my diet and learning about nutrition, although I was never over five pounds overweight, I felt a lot better. I started on the path to become a vegetarian and then almost completely vegan (I'll never give up cream in my coffee). I gave up meat first which was surprisingly easy and lived on chicken and fish. Chicken left next and fish a few years later. Salmon, the hardest thing for me to give up, and I gave it up more than once. I would see it in the supermarket freezer and walk to the cashier, by the time I got there my conscience would kick in and I would hand it over to the cashier.

Why? Hopefully not sounding too self-righteous, although there is some of that in it, I believe everything has a right to live, (as long as it doesn't hurt anyone especially me), it respects and helps the environment and importantly it is a very healthy way to live. The exercise benefit was more psychological than physical in that it allowed me to work out some of my anxieties in the water (which I always felt had a secure, womb-like feeling). I also found that exercise was a good anti-depressant and when I didn't do it for a few days, I would fall into a funk. It was as good for the mind as the body.

Fishlike, I swam all over the country in motels, hotels, rooftop pools, YMCAs, community pools, lakes, and oceans (if there was a puddle of water anywhere I was in it). I remember impressing a teen-age couple when swam in thirty-eight degree weather in a heated motel outdoor swimming pool. I had to explain to them that getting in and out of the pool in the cool air was the challenge not swimming in heated water. One time while swimming in a cold September ocean off Atlantic City a pod of dolphins swam right by me. (I noted their swimming ability was far superior to mine.)

I visited Vegas three times during my time with the union. Vegas is the flagship of the union with the biggest local and influence in the city's economy. Hanley was one of the five most powerful men in the city according to the local press. The union has had a long history of strikes and struggle against the corporate owners of the casinos (which are still continuing). Corporations have moved into a more dominant role in casinos, which at one time had a strong Mob element. There is a long history of Mob-related casino owners and managers interspersed with periodic murders.

The Chicago "Outfit" once had a big piece of the action in Vegas, skimming off casino revenue for the Mob. Tony (the Ant) Spilotro was the point man for the Mob until his erratic personality and outside criminal behavior alienated its leadership and led to his and his brother's murder in 1986. Spilotro asked for time to say a prayer before they killed him, he didn't get it and they beat him to death. I don't imagine he gave any of his many victims much time to pray either. I'm not a gambler, (beyond the office basketball pool winning or losing ten or fifteen dollars in a friendly card game), but I spent some time in the casinos just to get the feel of them.

The waitresses were attractive, the drinks free, the food good, and the action unrelenting. Walking into a casino in daytime was like going to the theater, one suspended a sense of reality. I found the themes of the big casinos artificial with a Disney-like quality although there were startling scenes such as having a drink in a bar with a large, live very colorful, tropical parrot, (it wasn't much of a conversationalist perhaps there was a language barrier.) I watched three oriental men throwing money around playing Baccarat and losing big time. Then saw three women who had picked the winning lottery numbers on their cards looking very sad when the waitress hadn't picked them up for the game. They impressed me with their forgiving attitude, gamblers seem to have a fatalism bred by tough experience.

It was recreation for some people. I saw scores of senior citizens dutifully dropping in coins into slot machines for hours. Buses would drop off loads of these people at the casino doors and they would move like cattle to the playing fields onto the casino floors. The circus atmosphere, and the excessive self-indulgence that came with it, going beyond escapism into hedonism put me off Vegas or more precisely the "Strip". It was a Disneyland gambling spectacle to me.

I digress: I got the uncut CD for Scorsese's Casino years afterwards but was so turned off by the constant swearing I tossed it. I'm not opposed to some swearing, sometimes it is the perfect emphasis to say something and I do it, but in my mind or when I'm around men who do the same. But there are limits. It reminded me of when I was in the Army there was a guy in the next room who couldn't do a sentence without swearing. I think he had a kind of Tourette's syndrome. Some psychologists say some swearing is a healthy emotional release. I buy that but too much must be a sign of unhealthiness. (So fuck it, let's get on with the memoir. :-))

I traveled up and down the West Coast either visiting or working in locals, making occasional forays out East to talk with local officers about the program. I had some nice experiences when living in Monterrey near the ocean and driving to work watching the sea otters play in the surf cracking open shellfish with a rock and enjoying their meal like sophisticated diners in a seafood restaurant. They were one of the few animals I have ever seen that seemed to genuinely enjoy the struggle for survival. The Monterrey local well run and straight as an arrow. Before I left, I walked another picket line on a hotel in neighboring Carmel. I'm sure Mayor Clint Eastwood didn't like it. I got into Chardonnay at the time sampling different California wines. I found Sonoma County wines the best and still do, red or white.

I learned there occurred a case of whistleblowing in the San Jose local in 1982 when a business agent told another Senate Subcommittee about the president Frank Marolda who spent union funds for personal use including hiring his brother as an armed bodyguard. I popped in on Marolda one day to ask about any interest in the computer program. He demurred. When I left I saw him come outside the office and watch as I drove away. I'm not sure he was convinced I stopped there about a computer program, (but that's the way these guys think). A business agent wrote Hanley about the problems at Marolda's local, informing him the union's assets had decreased over 50%. Hanley did nothing, they fired the agent.

I drove on to Los Angeles, San Diego, Santa Monica, Santa Barbara, and in San Francisco for a few months, I lived in North Beach while working on Local 2, one of the healthier and more democratic locals. I liked the climate of being in a local which was busy, progressive, smart; it made one respect what a union can be with dedication. The officers and staff were dynamic and took their work and the members seriously. While vocal differences between officers and segments of the membership happened, they all were united in their efforts to improve the life of the members. It would be interesting to do a sociological study how this big city union avoided organized crime dominance while others did not. It all seems because of something like tradition (or maybe just luck).

I took the trip to Alcatraz and found out that at one time there were so many Chicago Mobsters there they named the cell blocks after the names of Chicago streets like Michigan Avenue and State Street. I took a selfie of myself in a cell. I visited City Lights Bookstore, which seemed to me more yuppie than beat in style. I saw an exhibition fight between a local fighter and former middleweight champion Roberto Duran. I saw vomit and blood from the under-card fighters and decided to watch any future fights on TV where it appeared more aesthetic. I did the library and the art museum. San Francisco disappointed me, (I am the only person I know that doesn't love it), The weather was damp and cold, the culture overrated, living costs expensive and the city prettified but uncomfortable.

I moved over to Berkeley for the balance of my stay in the Bay Area renting a guest house in the picturesque hills. The main house and the guest house were architectural rich duplicates of a home in Italy that the owner, a dentist, had seen there in the Army. Walking through downtown Berkeley's Telegraph Avenue was like stepping back into the Sixties with pig-tailed guys standing around acting as if they were in a time warp. I was drinking coffee in my car in front of Peets, a local coffee house of some fame, when the Loma Pietra earthquake hit the area. The car started rocking gently like a boat on wavy waters and NPR clicked off the radio. My first concern was for my coffee, which I covered quickly with a lid. Looking out the window, I saw the lampposts swaying and people coming out of Peets. There was no panic, and I felt it was a lark.

A man in a car behind me walked over to my car. I laughed and said, "Now I'll have something to talk about when I go back East". "Yeah," he said, "but this was a big one". As a native, he understood the difference. Minutes later, when walking to the university, I saw hundreds of students pouring out of their classes. In one building a TV was on and I found out about the collapse of the Freeway and the damage to buildings in San Francisco and I understood it was not a lark after all. That night an aftershock got me out of bed and on my feet with an alacrity I didn't believe I possessed. The housing complex was badly damaged during the firestorm in Oakland in 1991. As beautiful as California can be, driving down the highway looking at the ocean comes to mind, earthquakes, fires, mudslides, drought, etc. are a dark side which helped preclude any thought in my mind of living there.

The aftershock, in fact, impressed me more than the original earthquake. Experiencing an earthquake is psychically and physically unsettling; It shakes one faith in the very ground one walks on, the stability of the earth itself. It takes some time to recover trust in gravity. However, I had no problem returning to the work the next day. The local's female president, who had a tough facade and swore like an infantry sergeant, was a total wreck. They told me the International had called to see if I was alright, a concern I treated with cynical amusement which she thought was rather odd.

I flew south to Dallas and Atlanta. The union like others had limited success in the anti-union South. Dallas' union had the sky chefs, (those workers who prepare those "fabulous" meals one eats on airplanes), at the big Dallas-Fort Worth airport. The union local had some good people, although one officer was double dipping on expenses collecting both from the International and the local. His secretary, who was blackmailing him, then reported him to the DOL, and he left the union. Atlanta, a small local, wasn't interested in a computer system. We agreed since some locals were too small to justify a computer system.

I was racking up frequent flier miles, living off the expense account, saving some real money for the first time in my life, not even maintaining a home apartment just moving from one city to another working. My expense account covered my food and rent, the two of the most major expenses in many lives so my check often intact, deposited into the bank. My address was the union or a post office box on the road. For tax purposes I had to declare some place as a home and I made D.C. my ostensible home which made some sense since it was also the home of the union. I told people my name was "Homeless Hugh".

I took some vacation time and joined a cruise up the Strait of Georgia by Vancouver, a great trip, saw and heard whales, stopped by deserted Indian villages and ate well. The cook was a good-looking blonde with a history of remarkable adventures for a young woman. She took some interest in me, (maybe because I was the only eligible bachelor on the trip) and one evening when we were all sitting around drinking stood up, started to sing holding a glass of wine and devoted the song to me moving around and standing in front of me while she did it. I found it rather silly and uncomfortable. It reminded me of some movies I've seen where the nightclub singer does a similar number for the male star. She was distant from then on.

I have to admit it was a very nice feeling to walk into a restaurant or a supermarket, order or pick out anything I wanted and know that it was free to me. Coming from a background where I had to beg for food from a grocer, it was meaningful. Most of my life I always had to come down to one of the cheaper items on the menu when I ordered in a restaurant and I had to regularly pass up the more expensive goodies in the grocery store. So it was a very luxurious, liberating experience to be on the expense account although my frugal spending habits still dominated my tastes and I often opted for the cheaper option.

There were a few personal expenses like alcohol, toothpaste, dry cleaning, and recreation that I had to pay for myself. I had this interesting insight one day when I realized, after many months on the expense account paying for my life's expenses, that I almost resented it when I had to pay for anything. It was a shock for me to realize I wasn't incorruptible; that, I too, could go over the line if I didn't watch myself. This made me understand the problems that happen to so many people in positions of power who have access to expense money and abuse that trust. I learned that the temptation is there, is strong and that none of us is completely secure from the possibility of corruption.

I didn't abuse it, in fact, I always kept myself conscious that it was the members dues that were paying my expenses. I never cheated, although given the International's casualness about expenses, it would have been easy to do so. Beyond the morality of it all I also understood that I had to be careful so that when and if I they found me out, they couldn't come back and charge me with anything illegal. I kept copies of all my expense reports.

Sometimes the loneliness of the lifestyle got punishing. There was this painful emotional void, no close contact with anyone, no one to talk to about my experience, not even much in the way of entertainment or outside stimulation. Except for casual contact at a local during the day, I had no social connections for months. My life was work and one empty hotel room after another. The pain was physical; so strong it could almost bend me over. I remember sitting in a rental car in a San Francisco parking lot, feeling the pain in my body and telling myself, "I've got to do something about this soon". I complained to Leavitt about the loneliness. "Why don't you get yourself a nice little package to travel with?" was his suggestion. While a "nice little package" might seem tempting on the surface, it wasn't my style to travel around the country with "a nice little package". And I couldn't continue to do my exploring with the package around.

I had one constant companion, however: Wolfgang, my faithful teddy bear, went with me every place. I got him as a gift from my former German girlfriend (I wondered at the time if it was a commentary on my maturity). I had animated conversations with Wolfgang (who was an excellent listener) on long drives out West. It was fun, I would extol on some point, make jokes and carry on with Wolfgang as if he were a person which it seemed like he was and it struck me how easy it was to slip back into childhood. In Long Beach, I had checked out of a motel and driven some distance away from the city when I realized I had forgotten Wolfgang.

I immediately turned around and drove back to the hotel. It worried me that a maid might acquire Wolfgang for her child or something. Arriving at the hotel, I sheepishly approached the desk clerk asked quietly if "the maid had found anything in my room". "Oh," she said much too loudly, "your teddy bear". A group of people turned around and stared. The smiling desk clerk presented me with Wolfgang. I thanked her, stuck Wolfgang under my arm and hurried from the hotel. I later learned, with some relief, that it was not all that unusual for men to have a furry little animal when they travel. I guess we never fully give up some things of childhood.

CHAPTER SIX:
MY SEARCH FOR THE PAPER BULLET

We take no delight in existence except when
we are struggling for something
- Schopenhauer

I spent all of my working days and most of my evenings exploring the people, the papers, the world of the union. Once in a while, I would get back into the International for a meeting and I would use the time to go shopping for information at night. I would often use a national holiday like Christmas or Easter to shop because I knew the International would be deserted. But it was always tricky because it was not unusual for officers or organizing people to come in at odd hours if out of town and just returning. There was a shower on the third-floor for use by officers. I always had this fear of somebody popping out of a doorway at 2 am asking, "What the hell are you doing here at this hour?"

I had my little routine worked out. I would wait until late either leaving the building then returning or staying in my cubicle. Sometimes I would sip coffee in a deli next door to the union until late in the evening watching the garage entrance, waiting until everyone left. The security system recorded comings and goings in the garage where one used a pass to get in and also on the outer rear door. The system picked up the pass number and the time in and out so it was better for me not to use those entrances and I avoided them when possible. But knowing the laxity at the International I figured they didn't track the ins and outs of the system even if recorded. I was right no one ever questioned me about my in and outs at odd hours.

I would check out the garage to see if the cars in the allotted parking spaces were empty. I knew some who parked in what space and what kind of car they drove. If it looked good. I would pick up some papers and take the elevator up to the second-floor where I would walk through the halls and check to see if the offices were empty, (and the restrooms). If anyone saw me, I would pretend to be looking for someone to give them a memo or to leave a memo on their desk. Then I would go back downstairs and wait for them to leave. Finally, I would go up to the third-floor and perform the same check.

It took discipline and patience, but it worked well over a long period and countless ventures into the files. I always copied the information I was interested in and never took originals. I would stuff the copies in my briefcase and leave. At first I kept the information in a safe deposit box but I quickly outgrew it and began to put in a large locked suitcase which I kept in a public storage unit with some belongings in nearby Arlington, Virginia.

I had some close calls in my "shopping". Sometimes on the third-floor going through the files when I would hear the elevator being called down and I would have to hustle down the stairs. I always made sure the elevator was on the floor where I was shopping so I would hear the elevator door close to go down when someone pressed the button downstairs and there be would time to escape. I had to learn when the cleaning service came in at night. I always made it a point to say hello and talk with them so they would be comfortable with my presence.

The downstairs copier was in an awkward place for me being very visible to anyone who came in through the garage door, (it is hard to explain making copies at 3am in the morning). What I did was put a piece of luggage near the copier. My excuse would be to say I was catching an early flight, and I had stopped by to make copies of something I had to leave for somebody right away before I left. The next day, I could say I missed the flight or a local officer delayed the trip. A poor excuse maybe, but better than nothing. Fortunately, I never had to resort to this rather transparent ploy. I also made copies of something innocuous as a cover for whatever I was copying and I would put those copies by the machine so I could put them on top of the real documents if someone suddenly came in and saw them.

Surprisingly, despite the hundreds of copies I made at the copier scores of times; I never got caught at the machine except one time by the janitor who,, didn't seem surprised by my being there at midnight. Another time an officer came in late one evening and heard the "beep" when I booted up a computer. Then footsteps walking around checking out the cubicles looking for the source of the noise. Fortunately, I was in my cubicle. It was one of the general vice-presidents, we exchanged hellos as he took a long look at what I was doing on the computer. I mumbled something about just coming into town (which in this case was true); he nodded and left, and as far as I know nothing came of it.

On another occasion, I was alone in the building searching through expense accounts on Thanksgiving when a secretary surprised me from organizing arriving through the garage door. She saw me sitting in the accounting department with a bunch of expense accounts in my hand. She was as surprised as I was. I know I looked startled and guilty. "Hi," I said, trying to appear casual. I saw her pause and look at the papers I had been reviewing, but then she smiled, said, "Hello." I forget what I said, something inane about the irony of having to work on holidays. She disappeared upstairs, and I put the stuff away for another day. My read on it was that she thought I was doing something slightly off limits but probably figured I was looking for my expense account and just passed it off and sometimes people don't want to know what you are doing.

It was surreal. One day in the office I glanced out on the street and saw a big black limousine parked by the building. It could have been a scene from a Scorsese movie. Two suited men standing by it, one an athletic looking black man and a dark-haired, short, stocky Italian guy wearing a dark cap. The suited black man was flipping a coin staring out at the street and the Italian guy was wiping the windshield. He put down the rag and walked over to the black guy and bummed a cigarette. The black guy gave it to him without looking at him. He lit up and walked back to the windshield. I wondered who the passenger was, where he was from and who he was visiting but I didn't want to ask anyone and never found out.

It just a day in, day out effort, (and night in, night out) painstaking, dogged search, reading document after document and letter after letter. The material I was gathering was very broad. I was not finding the paper bullet I so badly needed and wanted, (these people were very careful not to leave a paper trail and I didn't expect to find any "smoking gun" memos; I knew someone who claimed they created paper to clutter the trail) but what I hoped to do was to find a mosaic of facts from different sources that could provide a criminal lead. It seemed just threading through a labyrinth of endless paper with no final destination.

In shopping, I was learning a great deal about the union, and I was developing quite a database of information. I knew all the players and had a good sense of who the good guys and bad guys were. I was developing a knowledge of the systematic manner in which financial abuses occurred in the union and although most done under the cover of technical legality. Some of them were questionable under LMDRA but they weren't being questioned by anyone. Why the hell was I questioning things? What made me do things like this?

Studies on the characteristics of whistleblowers (Journal of Accounting Literature) showed that they are idealistic rather than relativists, have a perceived responsibility toward ethical issues, are serious minded, and have anxiety and mistrust about money. Females blow the whistle more than males but only if the whistle is anonymous, but early career or retired males blow it more than females. (I guess this make sense, you have little to lose early on and also when you have stepped out.) Belief that blowing the whistle will change things is an important element in their actions. Machiavellianism is negatively correlated with whistleblowing.

Anonymity by whistleblowers has been a point of contention with the obvious advantage of protecting the whistleblower's identity and obviating the fear of retaliation but lowering the whistleblower's information credibility. It also can make an investigation more difficult since it has to start without the benefit of questioning the whistleblower to get more information. The first whistleblower laws did not consider anonymity. Now, however, anonymity is acceptable under Sarbanes Oxley and other laws and some corporations find it acceptable.

Leaking, a practice more and more common these days, are anonymous but usually known to the people who get the leak, often the press. Employees working in national security are excluded from any protection even if the information disclosed isn't classified. Only internal procedures are allowed. If the NSA gets a complaint, they refer it back to the organization for internal procedures, leaving the whistleblower to hang by his/her thumbs. The WPEA, Whistleblower protection Enforcement Act tried to change that by allowing certain other venues for disclosure but was shot down by Congress. The tough penalties the government can impose on whistleblowers can defeat abuses from being revealed by potential whistleblowers.

I was into every file possible. I am compulsive enough to be meticulously thorough and there were few files that I did not get into and methodically check out. Recognizing this might be an invasion of privacy and unethical I rationalized it on the basis that I was a computer person and that I was exploring computerizing anything and everything. (A rationalization that really didn't hold up too well in daylight.) I decided the end justified the means. I wanted the truth of the union and I wanted to make a change. I would not worry too much about the borderline ethical niceties. The union officials weren't concerned about the ethics of their looting.

The routine was grinding, tedious, time-consuming, but there was always that ever present hope of an important find. Once in a while, I would find something interesting. One time I found that Hanley deposited a hundred thousand dollars into his personal bank account. I wrote the details and passed it on to Anderson. It excited me; I thought I had found something important; However, nothing developed and the government, as always, never tells you anything not even thank you.

I found an invoice from an electronic firm that told me Hanley had a $48,000 counter surveillance hookup on his phone to avoid wiretaps. Interestingly, he kept an autographed picture of the late Mayor of Chicago, Richard J. Daley Sr. in his desk. I found that interesting and even a little touching. What was becoming clear to me was this was a man who wanted to be important and to emulate those that he considered important. The problem was that he didn't seem to care how he became important and the people he might hurt while striving for that elusive goal. Hanley's desktop was spotlessly clean, not a piece of paper on it, perhaps a commentary on how much hands-on work he performed.

I reviewed the International audit reports of locals and the International. The reports were perfunctory. The auditors, untrained and uneducated in accounting principles didn't raise many corruption or malfeasance issues nor were they encouraged to do so. Friends of Hanley or employees who coveted the job wound up on the auditing staff often with no accounting experience or background. I remember one guy, a friend, of Hanley's who had joined the auditing staff, pondering something on his desk for almost fifteen minutes. He asked me how he could figure out what checks hadn't cleared the bank. It never occurred to him to look at the bank statement. Apparently he never balanced his personal checking account. I wasn't in the mood to help him; I never liked cronyism.

The International was highly political and friendly locals were unlikely to suffer unhappy consequences from an audit. There were many serious ethical issues at a number of locals that were never addressed. The auditors were very well paid, worked out their homes when not on the road, and had little supervision. They had a cushy job with few professional demands. Despite a requirement by the HEREIU constitution for an annual certified audit by a public accountant, many locals did not meet the requirement. The opportunity for financial abuses was golden for officers who ignored by-laws requiring informing members of salary increases, separation packages, and other benefits. I read the DOL audits.

The 1991 International audit found seventeen violations and criticized accounting controls. As I went over the correspondence between the DOL auditors, the union, and the accounting firm it struck me how the same accounting problems were referred to again and again over the years and how nothing was done by anyone to correct them. DOL after years of International stonewalling suddenly, laughably, became concerned that the "International was attempting to circumvent their directives", (only the government would take years to figure that fact out). However, even that belated realization didn't lead them to any action. The Department raised the issue of personal airplane flights and the lack of record keeping on the union's jet in a 1989 memo; The issue was still unresolved three years later when the DOL finished their audit of the International.

The gross ineffectiveness of the DOL shows through again and again in various reports. The Department asked for expense account documentation and repeatedly stonewalled. The DOL audits reflected a combination of bureaucratic indifference, ineptitude, and legislative impotence. I reviewed current expense accounts and went back into the microfilms on decades old expense accounts (and, interestingly, found that the only records missing were Hanley's expense reports from 1974 to 1977. That was when the government was looking at Hanley's tax returns. Tracking real estate transactions, looking at cost records on the airplane and checking on who used the motor home. I went through payroll records and computer printouts. I tried to find out who was using the luxury condo but drew a blank there; they didn't keep records. The bookings must have been done informally through one of the secretaries.

I went through payroll records to see who was making what and how much they got in raises. I pulled computer printouts on financial transactions from the IBM 36 computer; I had to read manuals to figure out how to do this one. I thought I had it down then I found out the computer kept a history of computer usage. Afraid the regular computer operator would know somebody was into the computer I then had to quickly learn how to delete the history of my entry into the computer, (not an easy task under time pressure) but I worked it out and deleted my record of entry.

I found out where the security man kept his keys and I got in there one night when I found the door unlocked (not a very good security man; he left shortly afterwards). I used them to get into locked file cabinets. I was very careful not to disturb anything and to put everything back where I got it from in the file. I wore gloves. Still, at least one staff member must have had suspicions because she put scotch tape on her unlocked file drawer so she would notice if anyone disturbed it at night. I replaced it when I was through searching.

I got in the habit of snapping a mental picture of an office in my mind before I started searching it and then after finished I would retrace my steps, stand at the door and try to see that same image in my mind. I admit to being uncomfortable with my clandestine efforts. I felt as if I were violating private space when I went through desk drawers and like an eavesdropper when I read personal correspondence. It just didn't feel right. One time as I went carefully through an office in the dark using my pen flashlight as a guide I thought to myself, "You little sneak."

Climbing through dusty storage boxes, I went through bundles of old telephone bills checking to see if Hanley had called any suspicious numbers. Even as I write this I am awed by the tenacity and dedication I had to the task, neither fatigue (I often only slept a few hours on the floor of my cubicle) nor fear slowed me down a bit. I never seemed to get discouraged. Some times, I would feel absurd. I would think it was grandiose to believe I could bring down a Mafia-inspired cartel. I always realized that I was a very small player who could easily be crushed caught between two monoliths, the government on one side and the union on the other, neither of which would care about hurting me to accomplish their goals. Somehow I had to keep trying, and I did.

It was strange. Roaming through the quiet empty building thru the night, listening for sounds, looking out the window when I heard a car stop or headlights flash on a window, opening file drawers, searching through file after file, reading and carefully replacing a sheet of paper after sheet of paper. I would make coffee and drink it throughout the night. (I had to remember to clean things up and turn the pot off when I left) Although I was often tired, I was so driven I had no concern about it. My passion to do something about the union seemed to possess me, making everything else in my life incidental. And I was caught up in my mission; I enjoyed the challenge, even the danger. I found a meaning in it I had never had before. I was on this long paper trail, this white maze of paper with numbers and words which somehow, someway I believed could lead me to my goal. It was almost the faith of a missionary believing in some kind of salvation.

I liked the role of a spy. There was this fragment of a song that used to run through my mind; "I'm on to something big," to this day I have no idea of where that line came from but it was there and seemed to motivate me. There was a quiet excitement in my cat-like nighttime prowling around the vacant offices of the union, an electric tension when I heard someone else in the building and a sense of relief and victory when I escaped. I was doing something risky and important, something no one else was doing. Somehow the spy role fit, snugly, comfortably like a favorite cap.

Caps. I wear caps, I have a repertoire of caps, various colors to match shirts, jackets, pants, etc. (being "color-coded" a girlfriend called it) I kept this habit (my security blanket) from Chicago days where. it's only academics and gang-bangers who wear them. One needs to be careful wearing one in gang territory. You can get some hard looks. Hats always seems to be symbolic. I always find it intriguing how a hat can change people's perception of you. I bought a rather expensive blue black fedora that I rarely wear but when I do, it seems I get instant respect. Funny.

The search was interesting beyond my efforts to find evidence of wrong-doing. I was seeing rather the multi-faced efforts it took to make organization exist; the endless chain of paperwork needed to run the day-to-day operations of a union, the efforts of hundreds of people in their memos and reports. Toward dawn light would come creeping, through the windows of the building and I would turn off the coffee machine, clean up, make sure I turned off all the lights I had turned on, pack my night's findings into my briefcase and stop the shopping expedition.

After finishing my "night shift" I would wobble out into the quiet Georgetown streets at dawn, go have breakfast up on Wisconsin Avenue at a diner, then turn around and go back in to work the day shift. I kept some clothes in my cubicle and would change my shirt or tie to avoid suspicion for wearing the same clothes two days in a row. I remember the newsletter editor doing a double take on me one morning when I didn't change and at some level he knew I was wearing the same clothes I had on the day before. He may have thought I was out all night but I made sure I changed clothes from that time onward.

I was vigilant, but I did not spend a lot of time worrying about what might happen to me. At one level I expected that eventually my luck would run out and I would get caught but at another level, I denied that eventuality. It was always hard to walk the ambiguous lines between being reckless, careful, and too cautious. I crossed all those boundaries at various times doing my covert work on the union. I rarely had to urge myself to be bolder, but there were times when I had to caution myself against being too bold. Besides the public interest attorney and my ex-girlfriend, I confided in no one no matter who they were or how much I thought I might trust them.

The ability I had to shut down my emotions I trace back to my childhood approach to dealing with the shock of rejection. I had learned to suppress my feelings ruthlessly then, and I used this ability to deal with the fear and anxiety that might have prevented me from doing what I was doing in the union. Candidly, I don't think I would have been able to do what I did without this ability. While very functional in aiding performance, there was a psychological downside to repressing feelings manifesting itself in depression, however, I was willing to pay that price.

I had casual connections with the personnel at the union. Most were pleasant enough. We made jokes, small talk and found some topics of mutual interest. I found a few people I knew were okay and made conversation with them. Most of the employees were not university types but people who had the skills and education of the average office worker. For many, but not all, I didn't sense much real dedication to the labor movement, and perhaps I shouldn't have expected that. Some longer term employees had an ingrained loyalty to unionism and were part of the union culture. They would participate in picketing local restaurants or hotels when called upon to do so.

When I was in town, most of the time I went up to a little historic garden on "M" Street and ate a takeout lunch. The chef took offense at this. "Why don't you eat upstairs with the rest of the staff" he asked. "I like to get out of the building and take a walk at lunch, " I said. That seemed to satisfy him. On another occasion he implied I had an "attitude". I always tried to be an innocuous as possible with the other personnel. I didn't want any complications getting in the way of my real work. One day I found out he was going to visit Greece, and I took him an article about Greece from the travel section of the New York Times. He went around afterwards telling people how I brought him the article. That was all it took to avoid a potential problem.

I took one secretary to lunch at the Georgetown Mall (the only Mall in America I like; It played Mozart at lunch and had a tasteful ambiance different from most modern malls). She picked up her sandwich, "Are you with the FBI?" She asked it in a casual, innocent manner as if she were asking where I went to school, as if she were making conversation. It startled me for a moment but then I laughed and shook my head, "No, I said, but would I tell you if I was?" She laughed, "I guess not" she said and started in on her sandwich. We went on to other things but I knew there were still either suspicions about me at the union or she was voicing old ones.

I ate up at the union's employee restaurant on the top floor once in a while when the weather was bad. There was an officer's section and one for the other personnel. There was a female assistant and the Greek chef who doubled as a chauffeur for Hanley, the assistant, attractive, of course. The food was good. Often one or two of the officers, rather than sit alone, would sit with the office personnel. This was my only real exposure to direct social contact with the other officers. There were one or two attempts to draw me into the circle. One time the General VP O'Hara asked me, "Do you drink Hughie?" It was an entrée into a drinking invitation. "Very little" I said. Although it may have provided me with some loose talk and leads, I didn't want to go through the acting that would have been required to maintain their trust. I didn't feel I could pull it off. I'm not a good actor or a good liar.

Leavitt one day called a meeting and pointed his finger at me: "I putting you, he said, "In charge of the computer program, get whatever help you need and get it done by convention time." Leavitt, despite his business and educational limitations, had some sense of progress and he was keen on the computer system. He was even warning us of the Y2K (Year 2000) problem and this was in 1990! He read my memos and took an interest in their content. Now, suffering from diabetes, Leavitt still continued to show up at the office every day. He didn't need to work for money he said, he just wouldn't know what else to do.

Leavitt had an old time lifestyle and a certain guarded warmth. He liked to go to the steam bathhouses, gamble at the track and travel. Married to a younger woman, his second wife, an attractive blond woman, (who didn't like to hear him called "Blackie") I heard he had a son, but he never talked of him. He would ask the accountants about their families and admonish them to take good care of them. He didn't like drug use, people who "got on that shit".

There was a couple of times he seemed to want to get close to me too, once asking me if I fished. "I've never caught a fish in my life, Herman" I said, and I hadn't. Another reason that I did not want to get involved with any officers was my belief that, by becoming friends with them, it would exacerbate the anger if they found out about my activities. I knew that becoming friends with them would just increase a stronger sense of betrayal and perhaps a stronger motivation for revenge. And I wasn't interested in having friends like that.

Because of my travels and Hanley's infrequent time at the International I saw and encountered Hanley only a few times at the International during my six years at the union. During my first year when I began to explore at night I was working late waiting for the office to clear out when Hanley and the security man were walking around the office. Hanley heard me in my cubicle. His voice was suspicious. "Who is that?" he said. He knew most union people are not ones to work overtime unless they are getting paid for it. The security man reassured him. "Oh, that's just the computer guy," he said. Fortunately, he didn't see me because that would have triggered his suspicions immediately.

My assistants were a mixed bunch and somewhat problematic given their respective personalities and relationships with the officers. There was widespread nepotism and cronyism at the International and two of my people had strong personal relationships with Leavitt, one a relative and the other a close friend. Some of them would conspire against me and one of them sent an anonymous letter to Hanley criticizing me. Hanley passed it on to Leavitt who passed it on to me. I dealt with them to get the job done, but the politics of the situation made doing an effective job of management impossible. I was also more interested in accomplishing my greater goal than doing my official job at the union.

I had been advocating that we hire our own programmer to cut down fees and Leavitt agreed. Then an idea came to me. I contacted Anderson and asked him if he wanted to put a federal agent in the union, someone I could hire as the programmer. "I think that's an excellent idea," he said. About a month later, I was meeting with the feds: a local organized crime supervisor, one of Anderson's people, the agent who would go into the union and a government attorney. We met in the evening to talk about it in a house I was renting in Arlington, Virginia. (I taped it, putting a tape recorder in a large palm plant near the dining room table. Figuring if they could tape me without my knowledge, I could do the same). I had almost as little trust of the Feds as the Mob and wanted a record of the negotiations.

The attorney's presence annoyed me. They had told me that the meeting would only be between myself and the agents. They were already playing games. I didn't make an issue of it. The local agent, a supervisor of some sort, was a tall gray-haired man who had the demeanor of a government official, neat, diplomatic, cautious. He looked up the stairway to the second floor when he came in as if he thought there might be other people up there.

The attorney who was supposed to be protecting the government's interests in the negotiations never said a word during the hour long discussion; He just sat there with a goofy smile on his face like this was something out of a Mob novel. They kept pressing me on what I knew, "let's lay our cards on the table," one guy kept saying. "Look", I said, "I'm not a professional investigator, I'm an amateur, you guys are the pros, if you put somebody in there you'll find something." They kept telling me how much work it required to put a plant in the union: "It's a big operation to put an agent in there, we need a wire, we need a backup, it's expensive, it uses up a lot of manpower." There were the usual suspicions, and the meeting didn't produce a decision to do it. They wanted something concrete to go after; they didn't want to go "fishing". They didn't care about the financial abuses or the membership's exploitation.

The aide to the Secretary of the Treasury called me in to his office that week, always an experience since his administrative style led to placing piles of paper on the floor, which often surrounded his desk all the way to the door. It forced one to walk zig zag through a literal maze of paper to reach a chair. He claimed he knew exactly where everything was and he could get it anytime he wanted. I never tested that claim, but I didn't believe it.

When I threaded my way through the papers, I sat down. Hesitating a moment, he always seemed uncomfortable dealing with me but then got right to the point." "The International doesn't like putting employment ads in papers with their name, they like to use a post Office box instead, (a tactic to avoid a government agent from answering it). He hesitated again: "They wouldn't like it if you hired a black person for the programming job". I nodded but said nothing but it amazed me that he would say such a thing out loud in that day and age. I promptly went out and hired a young Nigerian programmer. No one ever raised the issue; Leavitt went out of his way to indicate it didn't make any difference to him "I don't care what color you hire, black, white or purple" he said and I don't think he did. I liked that about him.

The aide, a small man with reddish blond hair and a hard face, was from Cincinnati (there were other office personnel who had followed the union to DC). He was Leavitt's administrative aide in the Secretary-Treasurer's office. He lived out on Chesapeake Bay with a male friend. Although he said he that he hated travel and did little beyond annual meetings and convention he would commute to work in a leased automobile. He told me one time he didn't even fill his gas tank and used "full serve". "I let them fill it up" he said. I didn't like that. Why couldn't he get his ass out of the car like everybody else? Thinking of members struggling to survive, the aide paying for full service on the union's leased car bothered me. He was making well over $100,000 a year, not bad for a guy with a high school education. The accounting partner didn't think much of his skills, "he's a nothing". he said to me one day.

CHAPTER SEVEN:
I GET SETUP

Of all the things to bear and grin, the hardest is being taken in.
- Phoebe Cary

Despite all the perks, there was considerable unhappiness among the employees in the Secretary-Treasurer's office. There was a strong consensus that there was a lack of leadership resulting in confusion and inefficiency at the working level. The lack of supervision led to people making their own rules which decreased morale and sometimes led to conflicts. Mismanagement affected my project because the Secretary-Treasurer's office thru his aide, maintained supervisory ability over my people, including okaying their expense accounts and raises. I told Leavitt, "Herman I can't supervise properly unless I have some say on raises; these guys will not pay any attention to me.". "You're right," he said, and he made the process to include my approval and recommendations week.

I didn't push on approving the expense accounts because I didn't want to challenge the aide's authority any further. My real goal at the union all the time I was there was not so much for the official work I was doing. I wanted to stay in there and get the evidence for the deeper change I wanted. I had two jobs and the unpaid one was the most important one. I wasn't going to do anything that might jeopardize that goal by getting involved in conflicts over power struggles and if efficiency suffered so be it.

Age and illness had diminished Leavitt's energy, and since he lacked a business education, he relied heavily on his aide, who had been around the union for most of his adult life and had worked as an assistant to John

Gibson, a prior secretary-treasurer who in 1980 was found guilty of conspiracy and embezzlement of union property. His aide had to testify at his trial," I don't want to do that again,", he told me. Singer Wayne Newton and comedian Danny Thomas testified as character witnesses for Gibson. Maybe they should have had character witnesses too. Gibson received his paychecks while in jail and honored for his prison gig by receiving a credit card, per diem of $40 a day, leased automobile, pension, and lifetime salary. The *emoluments of office* the documents allowing the perks called it. A reward for keeping his mouth shut during his prison term.

I had a low opinion of the International's accounting firm because I knew they knew of the rampant financial abuses going on in the union, that internal control was poor and did not meet accounting standards. Massey confided in me one day that he thought the union would spend itself into bankruptcy and wind up merged in another union, "They'll wind up merged into the Service Employees International" he said. Hanley had almost bankrupt the union in the Seventies with such unrestrained spending that it forced the union to downsize. (Hanley had also filed personal bankruptcy in 1961, prior to his rise in the union. Going bankrupt seemed to be his specialty.)

There was no budget, no payroll protocols, no written personnel procedures, no training manuals, no time sheets for organizers or business agents, no control over expense accounts and few standard business reports. None of the basic business practices necessary to run a financially responsible organization. I used to think a mom and pop grocery store had more financial controls. There was such a casual approach to the union's business affairs that it almost had a zany, comic appeal if one forgot the damage it was doing to the members.

There was a great deal of fat on the payroll evidenced by the fact that the International had 105 organizers floating around the union, three times more than the Teamsters Union which had over five times as many members. Noteworthy is the fact that the International's membership declined precariously over two decades despite the sharp increase in the number of organizers. There were 450,000 members when Hanley took over; that number dwindled to a little over 330,000 in less than a decade. Officer's salary expenses rose from $229,051 to $1,689,370 in that same period. Meanwhile, the union death benefit for members was a meager $200 and they hadn't increased it for decades.

I also sensed, a kind of disgust and disenchantment with some International people, who, although they didn't dare say anything, still left an impression they were unhappy with what was going on. (An exception to the rule of silence was the disgruntled shipping clerk who used to mumble sarcastically, "The members, who gives a shit about the members?") I especially remember a long-time union officer from a Midwest local. He was at heart a union man from the old school. I saw in his face a terrible disenchantment with the union that was eating him alive. He drank heavily at the convention. He died later that year.

But the general attitude was one of indifference. All the employees had to know of the union's notoriety because of the wide publicity but none seemed to feel any personal responsibility, they seemed to wear moral blinders. They bought Christmas and birthday gifts for the officers (something I stubbornly and stupidly refused to contribute to; I just couldn't bring myself to do it). Some seemed to think the Mob connection funny and would laugh about it, one secretary was said to have a music box with the theme song from the *Godfather*. As long as Hanley kept them comfortable with salary and perks, they didn't seem to care much about membership abuses.

Perhaps they believed they couldn't do anything about the financial caprices. More likely they compartmentalized their work from the abuses and pushed them into the background of their minds rationalizing that it wasn't part of their job description to do anything and it was none of their business. Maybe some of them just thought that was the way things were everywhere, (more likely they just didn't think much about it). The union was big on employee dinners, everyone would go out to a good restaurant, drink and eat and the union would pick up the tab. It kept most people happy if not fat.

I believe this attitude of "it's none of my business" is the indifferent individualism our culture fosters. We rarely care enough about injustice to act unless it affects us directly and then we expect everybody to care and only then do we act to correct it. We definitely, and to a point understandably, do not want to put ourselves at risk physically or financially. The general attitude seems to be that only a fool would put themselves at risk to change things. So what might be an act of conviction and they relegate courage to an act of foolishness or worse.

When someone blows the whistle, it creates a sense of conscious perhaps unconscious resentment, because at some level the other employees are challenged to consider whether they should have done something about the problem themselves and this can result in an unease bordering on guilt. The whistleblower has done something unusual, disturbed the status quo upsetting to all involved and resented. Conformity in the organizational culture is crucial to its smooth functioning even if that means smoothing over corruption. "Troublemaker" is the usual label sewed on to the lapel of the whistleblower both by his supervisors and his peers. And considered disloyal.

There is another very personal element involved in the whistle-blowing scenario that is ignored in the literature and that is the relationship factor. Suppose again you have a supervisor you like and have had a long satisfactory, even warm relationship with over the years, someone who has treated you decently and recognized your efforts. perhaps the relationship has extended out of the workplace into a more social one. Contrast this relationship with your working for a petty tyrant who is demanding, hypercritical and distant. Which one are you more likely to blow the whistle on if you discover ethical problems? And what will the relationships be like if you can continue to work in the organization? These are very tough personal considerations in the whistleblowing scenario. I'm glad I didn't have to deal with them.

Even those who go through the protocol of trying to resolve the ethical issue internally are seen as troublemakers, not problem solvers. People look for an ulterior motive believing that the whistleblower is hostile, trying to get even, is self-aggrandizing, self-righteous or worse unbalanced, a "crackpot". Being ethical to the point of a risk-taking action in the organization is an anomaly and regarded with suspicion, mistrust, and hostility. It isn't "normal" behavior.

The literature is replete with whistleblowers who have tried to correct things through internal processes and while they may have gotten listeners; they didn't get advocates or supporters. Nobody will go out on the organizational limb with the whistleblower. They *know* what will happen to him or her; The limb will break and she/he and the whistleblower will take a fall. In government the cliche on whistleblowing most often heard is "If you have God, the law, the press, and facts on your side you have a fifty-fifty chance of defeating the bureaucracy". Making the cliche "No good deed goes unpunished" more meaningful than ever.

One study by the University of Pennsylvania researcher, Patricia A. Patrick covered a fifteen-year period and examined 95 cases randomly and found 74 whistleblowers fired, 6 suspended and 5 transferred involuntarily. The rest given poor evaluations or demoted. For those that filed lawsuits, only 22% succeeded. Only 8 won damage awards, 2 were reinstated in their old jobs. Not a very rewarding scenario. Linking retaliation to the whistleblowing act is very difficult and is one of the critical things that courts should look at closely. The half-life of a whistleblower on the job is "nasty, brutish and short" (Thomas Hobbes description of life in the 17th Century).

There have been a series of legislative acts and 15 laws to strengthen whistleblower protections, including the mentioned WPEA signed by Obama in 2012. The Supreme Court has sided with whistleblowers 30 times in court cases before them. Whistleblowing is now a dynamic part of law. The public is more supportive of it. The National Whistleblower Center is a major player in helping them. Many government agencies have started whistleblowing policies. (There is now a National Whistleblowers Day on July 30th of each year. This is the day in 1777 when the first whistleblower protection act was passed by Congress because of retaliation against sailors punished for reporting the cruel misconduct of their commander in dealing with British prisoners. The struggle goes on 238 years later ("Nothing new under the sun").

Despite the dramatic progress, there are still serious holes in the legislation, including the right of whistleblowers to jury trials and due process. As always, it is the enforcement that counts most including the need for requiring mandatory punishment on supervisors when proven guilty of retaliation. 29 organizations have asked Trump to plug these holes. Good luck Whistleblowers! Trump has advocated rolling back whistleblowing protection laws, including the vital Dodd-Frank legislation on it. The Supreme Court in early 2018 diluted the protection for whistleblowers under Dodd-Frank. The Whistleblowers News Review lists recent cases and rewards and scores of the names of whistleblowers and their companies. Interesting reading not found in daily papers. I recommend it. (WWW.Whistleblowers.Org).

Federal employees have much more legal protection, if applied, than private employees (as you and I know), who can be fired "at-will" for any reason. This is true except for private whistleblowers who report violations of private companies of acts related to state or federal laws such as health and safety. Montana is the only state to eliminate the "at-will presumption". However, there are 59 federal and state laws on whistleblowing today, in 1959 there was one. A blanket federal law could and could/should cover all states. (In an ultimate irony a Trump whistleblowing protection group, the Office of Accountability and Whistleblower protection (OAWP) established to oversee the VA is itself being investigated for retaliating against VA whistleblowers.) The foxes watching the hens.

There was a situation where the Mob had gotten into a government safe to get a list of informants. I read where the government marshals didn't respect whistleblowers and considered them all informants either looking for money or revenge and treated them poorly in the Witness protection program irrespective of their motivation. I wasn't about to go into the Witness protection program.

The Mob hates informers above anyone else and makes no distinction between whistleblowing and ratting. Union peers considered whistleblowers as an aberration and in the labor movement as traitors to the cause, irrespective of the good they were trying to accomplish. They want to excuse any internal wrong doing as the means to a good end, notwithstanding the ethical issues. I've never understood this perverse loyalty to the "movement" rather than the people in the movement. It strikes me as high hypocrisy. Cover up and go along was the general style of many labor people (like their corporate counterparts). Blowing the whistle is considered a betrayal. Nobody likes whistleblowers, they're unusual, they're disturbing, they're trouble. The synonyms for whistleblowers in the dictionary are cogent, colorful, and representative, here are a few: canary, fink, rat, snitch, squealer, stool, stool pigeon, snoop, etc.

Author Peter Drucker and economist Milton Friedman were two corporate apologists who consider whistleblowing equivalent to "informing". The "Friedman Doctrine" says that the corporation's only social responsibility is to shareholders and profit not the public. Drucker and others consider whistleblowers as "rats", (funny this is a term the Mob uses also). Drucker and Friedman belie their grandiose reputations as market prophet and prominent free market economist with this repressive, short-sighted approach to whistleblowing. It should be clear to any intelligent observer that providing an internal outlet for whistleblowing in an organization makes much better sense than having employees go to the media or governmental authorities with their ethical issues.

Resolving problems in-house makes much better sense than in the public square. As one might expect from these two devotees of the bottom line, the concept of an employee being concerned enough with the public interest, whether that be health or safety, to go public after exhausting internal sources is incomprehensible. The "rats" Drucker and Friedman allude to are whistleblowers who have protected thousands of lives by bringing airline and nuclear safety issues to the public. This kind of rhetoric is amoral Capitalism equivalent to Mafia amorality.

But think about it. You're a supervisor in a corporation. One of your employees blows the whistle on some company practices which may or may not include you as being responsible. How comfortable are you going to be with having a person like that around your workplace? What does he/she does to the climate of trust in the organization? Won't you and everybody else start looking over their shoulders at their desks and wonder when the next whistleblowing going to be and who they will implicate? And the higher-ups in the organization won't they regard the whistleblower as an enemy in their midst and wonder what and who is the next problem? The whistleblower has broken the role in the corporate cultural code of a team-player, the "we're all in this together" credo. He or she has got to go or chastised so the code doesn't become meaningless. *Omerta*, the Mafia code of silence is as valued in corporate circles as it is in the Mob.

The subtleties of retaliation are limited only by the creativity of those offended by the whistleblowing. Unfortunately, in too many instances the

biblical injunction "The truth *will* set you free" holds up, it frees you.....
from a steady job, benefits and salary and maybe future employment in
the industry. There is an ethical protocol for whistleblowers which goes
something like this: (1) moral motivation as opposed to vindictiveness,
self-aggrandizement, maliciousness, etc; (2) using internal procedures for
resolving the issue before going public; (3) sufficient cause (4) sufficient
evidence of wrong behavior; and (5) a reasonable chance for success.
Applying this protocol to my experience I would have passed 1-3-4 but
not 2 and 5

In the summer of 1986, I met with Mike Anderson and two of his staff
in Chicago at Bannigan's, a Michigan Avenue restaurant/bar. I was excited
since I viewed this as a strong interest on their part. I was to work with
two agents, a man, and a young woman. We ordered lunch. I don't drink
during working hours but since this lunch was on the government. I
ordered a "rum and coke". The agents didn't drink. The male agent,
looking bored and snide, had a barely concealed contempt for
"informers". He had no notion of idealism as a motivation. The agent
was a type I found too often in federal enforcement circles, self important
with an immature romantic view of their work which must have been
garnered from TV programs and movies during adolescence. He was too
dense to distinguish between people who might inform for good or bad
motivations.

I decided right away I would not work with him. The young woman
seemed sensitive and sympathetic. We talked a little about the time I spent
with the IRS and then the subject switched to the union. "I'm hoping we
can do some good," I said. I still had concerns about the legality of what
I was doing and after lunch I turned and said to Anderson, "Maybe I
should get a lawyer". I saw Anderson's face change as if he suddenly had
an epiphany. It was only in retrospect that I realized that he thought I
wanted an attorney to protect myself from criminal exposure. I wanted
only wanted to make sure I didn't put myself at any legal risk to the union,
I wasn't concerned about my legality as far as criminal involvement was
concerned.

From then on, our relationship went cold I received very little input
from him and no guidance. The incident is revealing because it shows the
great fear the agents had about being used by the Mob. Informants who

were either loyal to the Mob or working as double agents (a la Jackie presser who is said to have played both sides as president of the Teamsters) had burned them. However, to me, it also revealed the rigid mindset of the investigator. Here was a man I had voluntarily agreed to help, whom I had written a letter waiving immunity and any compensation. He had checked my background, knew I had worked for the IRS as an agent and whom I had already given significant information. He still didn't trust me. One can't help speculating on the mentality of government agents so imbued with fear of bureaucratic criticism that they lack imagination and creativity, (characteristics their Mob adversaries have in abundance. Perhaps that is why they are usually a half step ahead of the Feds).

About a year later Anderson said the head of the Chicago DOL racketeering section asked about working with me and I began connecting with him. While more collegiate than the prior agent it was clear they had briefed him and he also maintained a guarded attitude. He was in his forties, earnest, very much a Chicago style guy, lots of street sense, gutsy. We met one time at O'Hare airport and he shared some concerns about various officials with me. Amid the background of the sight and noise from incoming and outgoing planes I told him as much as I knew at the time about my findings and impressions of the union people I had encountered. "I don't mind taking risks," I told him as we shook hands to leave, "but I want to take intelligent risks."

Afterwards, when I was out in California training one of my computer staff, a Latino who came from the Los Angeles local came to me one morning with a story. He was a swarthy, somewhat overweight guy who had a rather subservient demeanor. I was giving him a break by bringing him on the team to learn some computer skills. Blackie" Leavitt, he said, gave $10,000 to an officer of the L.A. Local running for election. This violated federal law. The story sounded strange to me, unreal, but I didn't want to pass over anything important. I called the DOL agent and told him the story with the caveat, "To take it for what it was worth.".

Some months later, I attended a staff meeting in D.C. in Leavitt's office. During the meeting I caught Leavitt glaring at me but said nothing then got up and left the room. "What's with him?" I asked. The aide shrugged, "He gets like that once in a while," he said. It took me a long-time, too long, to realize they had set me up, (I coupled my idealism with a tendency toward naivete creating a dangerous combination of characteristics.) The story had been concocted and passed on to me by the Latino guy who worked for me. I should have known better when he told me about the check since the guy was an obsequious type whose co-workers thought passed information to Leavitt. I blew it and it still bothers me to this day as I write about it. In my zeal, I gave it to the DOL, and the DOL had gone in looking for the fictitious 10k and they hadn't done it subtly. They hadn't worried about giving me much cover.

Blackie now knew I was an "informant". This is one more example of how little the government cares about protecting informants. They could have gone into the union on any pretext and kept my role secret instead they hurried in looking for the ten grand blowing my cover. Leavitt knew and I will never, ever understand why he didn't get rid of me. That would have been the prudent thing to do (that's what I would have done). He could have done it under any pretext for any reason. Perhaps he liked the cat-and-mouse game but it might have also been he had no fear of criminal involvement. The lucrative perks of the job were all authorized under a legal protocol that legitimized everything they did in the union. Another angle is that he didn't want Hanley to find out he had hired an informant since Hanley had told him he was "responsible for me". I'm reaching, but maybe he wanted me to nail Hanley and take-over the union. To this day I can't figure this out, it makes little sense but lots of things didn't make sense in this union.

Some months afterwards, Leavitt and I went to lunch in Georgetown. As we started to leave the office I picked up my briefcase. "You need that?", he asked, nodding to the briefcase. I realized he was worried about a wire. "Not really," I said, "force of habit." I brought the briefcase with me anyhow. I figured if I kept the conversation on the up and up it would reassure to him. At lunch we made small talk, but he told me about some health problem he had been dealing with. I felt sorry for him, this grandfatherly old man struggling with diabetes and now another condition. I found myself giving him advice on how to take care of himself, something he probably didn't need, but seemed to appreciate. There was something accepting, non judgmental about him that was appealing to me. It was as if he had this philosophical world view where everything that happened was okay, was the way it was and nothing else. But that was as close as I ever got to Blackie.

I decided not to work with the Chicago DOL agent anymore; He suspected me too, and I contacted Ron Chance, a DOL agent who had spent a career on some HEREIU locals, especially the Atlantic City local. He had testified at Congressional hearings related to the union. This agent was a welcome change from the prior agents: he was open, straightforward and dedicated. Chance, who worked as a highway patrolman before going into the DOL Racketeering Section, came out of Jesuit background and was incapable of dishonesty. He was around my height at six feet, trim and had a crew cut. I felt comfortable with him and over time we developed a mutual trust that was productive. We exchanged information with ease and confidence. He had limits on what he could tell me but he shared confidences when he could. Chance played a large role in driving out corruption from the Atlantic City local. He has since retired from the DOL.

CHAPTER EIGHT

"When all's said and done, all roads lead to the same end. So it's not so much which road you take, as how you take it."
- Charles de Lint

I flew back to Philadelphia and started arrangements for one of my assistants to put that local on computer. One local officer was a loud-mouthed ex-bartender who seemed to need to talk in two octaves higher than anyone else. One day he was loud mouthing an African-American member who promptly decked him right in the office. The business agents all ran out to break it up, but I didn't move from my desk. I felt he richly deserved it, and if they called the cops, I would back up the black guy. They let the man go and loud mouth gave me a look as he walked back to his desk. He saw I hadn't made the slightest effort to help him.

One memory I have of Philadelphia was checking in at the Hershey Hotel downtown with the clerk handing me a Hershey bar along with my room key; I thought it was a cute touch. When I went back to D.C. where I had parked my car, I found someone tried to break into the trunk. (probably Grogan who was never too subtle) The lower part of the trunk was bent as if someone put a crowbar in it and tried to force it open. Someone thought I had something interesting in the trunk. Clearly I was still the subject of some suspicion in the International. It was rather odd that I took incidents like this one in stride. I had settled into a kind of "catch me if you can" relationship with the union. I understood that some of them knew I was not to be trusted. It was almost a game but a potentially deadly one for me.

I drove to Baltimore, Saratoga Springs, Albany, and New York City. Baltimore was uneventful, the President, a large rather philosophical man, told me about drinking with Grogan. "Not a pleasant guy when he's drinking," he said. I had this curious exchange at lunch with an African-American agent who told me that there were no street gangs in Baltimore, when I doubted this, he got a little upset. (I hope he watches the *Wire* sometime in his life.) Saratoga Springs was cool: a small town, 26,000+ with lots to do: National Museum of Dance", the historic Saratoga Race Track which is what I imagine is stepping back into the 1920s. Art galleries, a casino, annual first class symphony orchestras, and the noted Skidmore liberal arts college (Is this sounding like a Chamber of Commerce ad?). It was a welcome respite from the dullness of other locals.

While in Albany, I met with my former girlfriend from Chicago. I first met her at a single's dance in 1983 when she was just coming off a divorce from a long-term marriage. She was an attractive, charming German woman in the mood to do something dramatic; ready to leave her old life and former husband to find and make a new life. She'd been married for some 20 years and needed a lot of support which I tried hard to provide. I think that was the basic motivation for her relationship to me. I always recognized that need and took her proclamations of love for me with some reservations. That proved out. But there was something of a romance and a bond that developed despite the mutual limitations. She was an art therapist given to psychological thinking and off-the-cuff analysis of my behavior. Having had my share of therapy, I found that easy to understand and deal with most of the time. She was also intelligent and a lot of fun. She was helping me emotionally, too.

For some time I'd been feeling somewhat provincial having lived, except for two years in the Army, all my life in Chicago and I was thinking about living somewhere else for a while. I' taken a trip hitting a few cities in the southwest and west thinking of leaving but came back and settled back in. She provided the catalyst I needed to make the move out, and we left Chicago in September 1984. We traveled for a year putting 17,000 miles in a 1974 motor home traveling, first out West, and then deep into Mexico. We had some adventures, the most harrowing because of our dedication to seeing the whale migration on the Baja. Seeing none on the beach but hearing them in the distance by a small island we took a Kmart vinyl raft out about half a mile to it and did see a couple of whales.

We basked on the island and returning found the tide had radically changed and was pulling us toward the Pacific Ocean. The raft was filling with water and we rowed and bailed like hell. With movie-like romanticism, I started to say that "Whatever happens I'm glad we had our relationship" She cut me off abruptly, "Row" she commanded and I did. We got back exhausted but more bonded than ever. Before leaving, we went to check out the salt flats nearby. It got dark quickly, and we were lost. Driving around aimlessly looking for a way out, we stopped the only other vehicle we saw. When I asked in English which he didn't understand, he said, "No conduzcas, muy peligroso." I knew the word peligroso meant dangerous so I got the message. "Don't drive, very dangerous". I pulled over by a small red shed and went in. I saw it had a few oily, wet rags hanging on a piece of wood. I figured someone would be there the next day. We slept and the next morning set out then I saw that if we had continued on another 50 feet, we would have fallen right into the ocean off the pier. We found our way out with relief.

Afterwards, we traveled around mainland Mexico for a few months and then back in the States, in North Carolina, we separated and parted on friendly terms when she found a job. I went to D.C. to work at the union. We understood we would separate when we started the trip but with one exception got along well during a year when we spent 24/7 together in what was effectively a nineteen foot Mobile box. No small accomplishment.

We rented a cottage in the Adirondacks and enjoyed a weekend, talking and watching black bear cavort outside the picture window of the cottage. We no longer made love. I never married (carrying on a long tradition of the Irish who still have 26.3% of males in Ireland single at 40-49 according to the 2016 census). I dated but not for a long duration. My childhood left me with little faith in love or the success of relationships, (this was more an emotional response than the intellectual one which subscribed to a belief in both). And I had a virulent fear of rejection which led me to escape out of a relationship at the first hint of that eventuality. I liked kids and done some tutoring with inner-city kids from Chicago's notorious Cabrini Green Housing projects but I never seriously entertained fathering one myself. I believed I would reject any boy the same way I was rejected even if I made every effort not to do it. It was a psychological heritage: my father's father rejected him, he rejected me and I didn't want to carry on that sick tradition.

When she settled in, I said, "I've got to tell you something." Then I told her about my work with the government. I told her because I wanted someone close to me to know about my "avocation" in case something happened to me. She accepted it as I knew she would. "Okay," she said. I realized it was foolish not to have someone aware of my role and since she was a therapist, she could keep a secret and she did. She had a dream that night. "They came after me looking for you," she said, about the dream. I felt bad about upsetting her but I knew her well enough to know she had the courage to deal with it. I was careful not to let anyone know about my relationships and I told her that. I didn't even keep names in my pocket notebook and everything important in there was in an improvised code only I could understand. I never talked about relatives or friends, (a local officer described me as a "very private person").

We kept in touch by letters for some time after that meeting. She remarried and moved from my area. We are still friends. I recently went to her husband's funeral, and she appreciated that. I visited her in the mountains of North Carolina after the funeral, and she seems to do well. She has strong relationships with her sons and several new and old friends. She will do all right. (In fact, she read the draft of this book and graciously made no comments about my interpretation about our relationship.)

New York was always divided up between the five crime families: Gambino, Columbo, Bonanno, Lucchese, and Genovese. I don't know which of them had the HEREIU locals there. Locals 100 and 6 had their own computer systems and expressed little interest in the International's program. Some Mob influenced city locals like 450 in Chicago, 226 in Las Vegas and New York didn't want anybody they didn't know personally coming into the local for any reason; they were that secretive. I didn't get a chance to look around in those locals and to my disappointment blew me off. I wanted to spend time in New York just to experience more of the city and scout out the locals. I had talked with Leavitt about going into the New York locals and he suddenly became very alarmed. "You're not going into Torrio's local are you?" I had no idea and still don't know where that was or who he was, but it was clear it was off limits territory. I said "No" and the conversation went on.

Back in D.C. I connected with an attorney, Art Fox, who had worked out of Ralph Nader's public interest network. Nadar might have pioneered whistleblowing when he blew the whistle on the automobile industry, in fact, he wrote a book on it in 1974. Fox had considerable labor experience and was on the advisory board of the Association for Union Democracy, a Brooklyn located union watchdog group. Their mission is to keep unions honest and as the name implies, democratic. A rare brave voice telling it like it was and is in the labor world. The founder, Herman Benson, was a protege of the respected Socialist thinker and leader Norman Thomas, and has spent a lifetime fighting union corruption. I contacted AUD who weren't able to provide much help on the union who they thought (correctly) had no viable dissident group in the membership to provide opposition to Hanley. I'm a subscribed lifetime member.

They were much more absorbed in the effort to rid the Teamsters of corruption (and had considerable early success there) with Teamsters for a Democratic Union. The TDU after a decade of effort elected Ron Carey a reformer as president. I found out some time later he had received hundreds of thousands of dollars in illegal campaign contributions and they ousted him from the presidency and the union. Hoffa's son James was elected president, a tragic ending two decades of reform effort. The moral: even the good guys can do bad and/or dumb things. Fox provided me with a sympathetic ear and some moral support, but essentially I found I was on my own in this Quixote mission.

I flew to Toronto to get a system set up there. The local had been using a "consultant" who was leasing them a computer and doing their reports at an outrageous cost. This scam was a popular one at some larger locals. I suspected one of the New York locals did too. I found and copied documents detailing the arrangement and what looked like the complicity of the Vice-president of the local. We got into a shouting match (which wasn't too cool on my part). about the cost of the computer system "You're screwing your members" I yelled. "You're a joke," he said, and stalked out of the room. Later I checked his office again and all the original copies of the documents gone but it was too late, I had turned over my copies to the government whom I understand turned them over to the Canadian authorities. However, nothing ever came of it, a conclusion that was all too common with law enforcement on labor fraud and which contributes to cynicism and discouragement.

One lasting memory I have of the local is that of the Haitian clerk standing at a window staring down intently at the street three stories below, at a cop putting a ticket on a car, "What are you doing?" I asked. She never looked at me and remained looking fixedly at the cop. "I'm putting a curse on this cop who's putting a ticket on my car," she said with all seriousness, continuing her voodoo stare.

The accumulated efforts of spending so many hours searching through the endless stream of papers that filtered through the union, copying documents, the thinking and planning coupled with long hours working on the accounting program days and shopping at night was overwhelming. It was like working two full-time jobs. I was trying to change things single-handed, and the task was formidable. I was trapped by the need to be absolutely discreet about my activities and the need for support and help. I trusted only myself. Attorney Fox told me one time, "You can't do this yourself." he was right, but I continued to play it alone anyhow, that had always been my style.

The tension of my efforts and the lonely, isolated life of continuous travel was draining me psychologically. I was a constant stranger wherever I was and always on guard. I was never adept at making quick friendships and I had no real social life. I worked late or pursued my now, my singular obsessive search for the elusive paper bullet that would pierce the heart of the corrupt International administration. In 1990, I was losing weight and looking and feeling bad. I remember looking in a mirror one morning at a very tired looking human being.

Some people remarked on my deteriorating appearance. The constant tension and stress along with the long working hours running me down physically and psychologically. I had concerns about my motivation and my almost fanatical dedication to whistleblowing. I had examined my motivation at length and had at different times come up with various interpretations, some flattering and some frankly unsettling. I was idealistic, but there was some question whether that was a virtue or a fault. I liked to think of myself as a realistic idealist but the whistleblowing challenged that image. Here, I was running around the country spending my life rummaging through file drawers every possible hour, reading documents, sorting through papers and running off copies of anything that looked like it might be important. I was risking both my physical, psychological and financial life on what was so far a fruitless crusade and which was likely to remain that way.

Who was I to think I could change an entrenched Mafia subsidiary, an organization that had powerful and influential politicians as allies along with leading clergymen on its side? The late Cardinal Bernardin of Chicago gave Hanley the Rerum Novurum award for his "Contributions" to the church and extolled Hanley as "A great labor leader". Bernardin also gave a speech at the 1996 convention, conveniently ignoring any past or present charges of corruption in the union.

The Catholic Church's relationship to the Mafia and the Mob both in this country and Italy has been an interesting one, condemning it publicly, but not hesitating to take its money or cozy up to it when expedient. The Church had no reservations about burying Al Capone in a Catholic cemetery in Chicago (a privilege they used to deny to a tragic suicide). The Church got creative with the death of John Gotti in prison. Gotti, convicted of five murders, could have a mass for the dead (but not with his body in the church) and to be buried in a Church crypt. Hanley gave big-time to Catholic causes even having a well-paid chaplain at union events, (a brother of Vice-President John O'Gara). The church's highly visible association with the union leadership gave it a credibility to the public it didn't deserve.

I pondered my motivation. Could it be just a crazy obsession? An acting out of some "B" movie plot I had seen as a teenager? Was I like Don Quixote wanting to live the life of the books I had read? Or was it a big ego trip looking toward recognition and acclamation at the end of the trail? Perhaps even hostility toward authority? While I was in Canada, I decided to see a psychiatrist. In retrospect, it is interesting that I saw a psychiatrist voluntarily since not long ago it was commonplace for government whistleblowers to be required to have mental examinations. There are, in any population, people who act out of mental illness, but it is a damning commentary on our society that people trying to do the right thing are considered abnormal. If you act ethically in our country, you are suspected of being mentally disturbed.

Donald Ray Soeken, a former U.S. Public Health Service social worker has written a unique, compelling, and revealing book "Don't Kill The Messenger" which tells the stories of whistleblower experiences. He realized in his work that the people he was interviewing were not mentally ill or "unfit for service" as the government like to label whistleblowers at the time submitting them to "fitness for duty" psychiatric exams. It reminds one of the old Soviet Union's method of dealing with dissenters by putting them in mental institutions for "reeducation" and/or long-term confinement. Soeken's role was to determine if they were unfit for employment, along with an expectation that would be proven. Soeken found only two people who had serious psychiatric problems during time at the agency. Realizing this bias, Soeken left his job and started an organization to help and support whistleblowers called Integrity International.

Soeken became a powerful advocate for whistleblowers helping thousands of them in every way possible over 25 years. What follows are excerpts from his book: Despite their contributions to society and the suffering they endured in doing it I'm sure that 99% of people have never heard of them or wouldn't have unless Soeken wrote his book. That is the paucity of recognition that whistleblowers receive. (A list of known whistleblowers and their very interesting experiences is on Wikipedia), read it at your own risk (of cynicism).

Steve Agee, a physicist at the Morton Thiokol rocket boaster plant which worked on space shuttles, In his work he found numerous flaws and errors creating safety hazards which he dutifully reported to higher management but received no response. Increasingly frustrated and concerned he went to the FBI which enlisted him to do undercover which he did compiling documents evidencing his concerns. Then, suddenly the case collapsed at the highest levels and Agee was the whistleblower out in the cold. They terminated him. He left for Australia to escape any retaliation and filed a wrongful termination lawsuit that failed. His marriage also failed. He resumed working this time for the government and finally retired to New Zealand because of health issues he attributes to the stress of his experience.

Russell Tice worked for the National Security Agency and discovered what we all know now that the Agency was conducting domestic spying on U.S, citizens without warrants . Tice agonized over his discovery torn between his NASA oath of loyalty and the clear violations of the Constitution's Fourth Amendment and tried to work within the Agency to no avail and went to Congress. This resulted in a long series of abuses: a psychiatric test, (which diagnosed him with a paranoid disorder and obsessive-compulsive disorder despite having passed his annual psychiatric test nine months before). Then, surveillance by the FBI, threats, denied access to his records and some agency facilities and assigned to a warehouse doing physical work. When he continued his efforts with Congress they removed him from employment. He lived and supported his family on unemployment insurance and part-time jobs. Virtue was its own reward for Russell Tice but virtue doesn't pay the bills.

So an interesting psychiatric paradox arises. If the norm is to act unethically, then to be ethical is considered an aberration. I remember an audit I performed in Chicago for a small north side accounting firm. The client was a psychiatrist who had gotten into trouble with the IRS for not reporting income. One of the audit tasks is to confirm accounts receivable which involves finding out who owes the doctor money and sending out letters to them to confirm that was true and the amount is correct. I went into his office and told him what I needed. He offered me a seat. He was a handsome man, soft-spoken, charismatic. "Sit down," he said warmly.

I said, "I need to review your receivables as part of the audit". He didn't look up "I can't give you my patient receivables; for legal reasons I can't reveal their identities. It's a matter of patient confidentiality," I knew this was a legal maneuver that didn't really hold up under closer examination. Accountants are also bound by confidentiality and this would have protected his patients. I reported his comments back to the CPA firm and proceeded with the audit. I left the CPA firm afterwards when I found that every audit I went out on involved someone was in some kind of trouble. (Including a business I had referred to IRS Intelligence when I worked for the IRS). They were taking clients that other firms wouldn't touch and charging them higher than usual fees for the favor. They also did one of the big Chicago Teamster locals, a very small firm doing a very big local.

An interesting aside was that I had heard a lecture by this psychiatrist a few years before in his large home in the Chicago "Gold Coast" area. (he had married an heiress). Standing on the stairway, he gave a low key impressive talk on Existentialism in psychiatry. I was exploring Existentialism at the time reading Sarte, Camus, etc. It seemed like a pragmatic philosophical approach to life. It became popular but passe after a while as so many psychiatric fads seem to do. The psychiatrist sentenced to jail for 90 days and then placed on probation. Sometime later I heard him on public radio, He was running a methadone clinic telling an interviewer he believed "A man who is too honest is out of step with his society". Doesn't seem he learned anything from his experience.

What this view implies about the ethical standards of our society is staggering; It says ethical behavior is abnormal; to be unethical is normal, in tune with an unethical society. Motivation isn't always pure or clear. Sure, some employees blow the whistle out of self-interest, not public interest. There is the whistleblower angry at his supervisor, one who is seeking publicity, who is protecting him or herself from charges of complicity in the wrongdoing, etc. Almost two-thirds of whistleblowing complaints in one survey dismissed for lack of evidence, so evil like beauty is also, in the beholder's eye. But that hardly makes whistleblowing abnormal, not unless wanting justice is also abnormal.

I made an appointment with a Toronto psychiatrist named Tom Verny who had gained some fame in the Seventies with a book on the psychology of unborn babies. Verny had his office in an old house in Toronto. He was around fifty, bearded, thoughtful, very much the common image of a psychiatrist. I talked to him about my background, family, and fears. We talked for a while of my relationship with my mother and father, (touching on the Freudian Oedipal complex relative to my relationship with them). I told him of my whistleblowing on my father,"Maybe it was an Oedipal thing and I was trying to eliminate him as a competitor for my mother's love." I said. (I was into Freud at the time). He sort of shrugged in a kind of "who knows" gesture. He wasn't too Freudian. I did tell him something about my non-profit work in Chicago, saying I had Socialist tendencies. I told him of the painful loneliness and unhappiness I was experiencing.

He listened attentively, with brief comments. Dr. Verny believed in taping the sessions and giving the patient a tape so he or she could review it. He believed these tape reviews could be beneficial to a patient. After the second session, Dr. Verny gave me two tapes. Upon leaving, I told him I had "something interesting to tell him next time" (meaning the union affair). Next time, never happened as his schedule and commitments to other patients under the Canadian method of universal medical care put me on the waiting list (perhaps because I was not Canadian) and I had to move on to work another local. I remember looking at the tapes and thinking I should get rid of them but I kept them with my cache of union documents in the luggage bag in a storage unit. I thought they might be helpful and/or interesting to listen to then. It didn't work out that way.

CHAPTER NINE:
I'M DISCOVERED

When we have just gotten out of the way of a vehicle,
we are most in danger
- Nietzche

A year later, I was staring at this same bag ripped open in my Arlington Virginia storage unit. At first I thought it was just a random break-in, someone robbing storage units. But when I realized what they took, I knew it was the International's work. My tapes gone, some documents and a small pair of binoculars (which must have appealed to the thief, maybe he was taking it for his kid), nothing else. I remember thinking, "This is like some dumb "B" movie plot except I'm in it". I wanted the break-in on record so the manager called the police but I said nothing about the union.

They didn't break the lock on the door of the unit (showing some professional expertise) however, someone had slashed the bag open. The thief left behind a flashlight, which to the cop's chagrin, I had picked up, contaminating it. However, the thief wore gloves and later the police determined that there were no prints either on the flashlight or the batteries. I said nothing about organized crime connections deciding to notify the Feds rather than involve the local police.

I drove back to my hotel suite in Georgetown and tried to reconstruct what happened. I opted to come back to the International about three months earlier to do some administrative work and to do some serious "shopping". I was also reaching the point of do or die, a state born out of frustration, exhaustion, and internal pain. I grew somewhat reckless (and felt it at the time). I had my things shipped to the International before putting them in storage, alerting them to the fact I was using storage. I began to do all night searches at the International again, bringing in food, sleeping on the floor in my cubicle, spending nights searching.

And then the flash point occurred. My Nigerian programmer told me he thought someone had tampered his computer with, someone had tried to enter it. I got too cute, too clever for my own good. I seized on the opportunity to make myself look loyal and allay some suspicions I knew existed about me. I wrote a memo describing the incident and showing my concern for security. It was a ploy that backfired.

Three days later Herman called me out to his plush Beverly Hills office. He sat behind his large desk in his spacious office, a long large picture window framed him against a panoramic view of the city. He looked at me hard. I could almost feel his concentration. "Edward", he began after a while, choosing his words carefully, "is very concerned about this.... incident with the computer because he thinks it might involve the government". "I am too Herman, and that's why I wrote the memo." It was a transparent lie. He continued, "Do you have any idea who might have broken into the computer?"

I sensed he was toying with me, feeling me out, that the question he was asking was not the one on his mind. "No, I don't", I said, "it could be someone just fooling around on his computer, could even have been the janitor, that's the problem we don't know". Toward the end of the conversation, he leaned back in his chair measuring me, I looked into his eyes; black, piercing and very thoughtful. I knew he didn't believe a word I said.

I told myself I had to be careful, and I tried, but I still took unnecessary risks, (In retrospect I think I may have wanted to get caught to end the ordeal). The long night searches at the union continued. One Friday, I called the storage unit from my office phone asking them if they would be open on Sunday. I had never used the office phone for anything "sensitive" since the wiretapping incident. I had always made such calls from payphones. I had been suffering from a herniated disk for two weeks I was rolling out of my bed, crawling from the bedroom to the bathroom. On Sunday, I decided to go to Georgetown Hospital's emergency room. I wanted to get some blank checks from my checkbook first and the blank checks were in the storage unit.

Sunday morning, I was driving out of the International garage where my rental car was parked to go to the storage warehouse. I don't know if it was the accumulated pain, the medication I was taking, or the unconscious desire to get caught, but I remember seeing a man in a white van react when I came out of the garage onto "M' street. I saw the van behind me on 28th Street as I drove to the 14th Street bridge. Everything seemed to be in slow motion and my mind was recording it like a video camera but not making an interpretation of the events. At the storage unit, I found my checks. I remembered I had made no audio notes on my tape recorder since I came back to D.C. in January and I picked up the pocket-sized recorder and began talking into it.

I had made tapes like this periodically for most of the time I was investigating the International. I realized it was a rather dangerous exception to my usual disciplined approach, but I wanted a record of my adventure, something for old age reminiscences. (I still have a few tapes and it's getting close to reminiscing time). I had gotten in the habit of recording tapes while on my motor home trip. I was obscure on the union tapes only obliquely referring to my explorations. However, the tapes also included the one I had made of my meeting with the Feds.

Early on, I kept copied documents in a safe deposit box but the volume drove me out. Just starting recording that day when a tall athletic man with unruly black hair wearing gloves and carrying a flashlight walked by the unit and looked in as he did so. I had talked into the recorder about two minutes when the man passed again going in the other direction and looking over his right shoulder into my unit. I remember feeling uneasy, but I passed off the incident. I talked briefly into the recorder and then put it into the bag. I closed the bag, locked it up and left the unit with the checks.

About a week later I took the elevator up to the restaurant on the top floor of the International for coffee one morning and joined about five other staff of the International sitting around a small table. There was complete silence when I sat down. The air was dense with hostility. I threw out two conversational offerings, but it was clear there would be no takers. I postulated it might have been the memo. Could they have been offended by my criticism of security? I thought of the experience in terms of office politics.

In the meantime, I learned Herman Leavitt made a surprise trip to the International from California. One of the staff laughed. "He didn't even tell anyone he was coming," he said. I saw Herman near the accounting department on the way to lunch. He stood in the doorway looking at me; we said nothing to each other. I understood the morning's oddness in the context of the unit burglary. *The word was out at the International that I was an informant.*

But my back still hurt, so I wobbled over to Georgetown Hospital and got an epidermal shot that worked like magic. Back at my suite, I tried to figure out what to do. I was only 3 blocks from the International and I felt very vulnerable. *They knew*, and I had to go to work there Monday morning! My brother for some unknown reason, (he nor anyone else in my family knew of my extracurricular activities) had given me a 22 pistol about two years before. I took it at the time although I am not a gun person but it had occurred to me it might be a good thing to have around just in case. It had languished in storage but now I wanted it. I drove back out to the unit and got the pistol.

Returning to the suite, my heart jumped, there was a noise coming from my room. I grabbed the pistol and looked desperately for the exit stairs. I cursed myself for not knowing where they were. There was more noise from the room. Would they be that indiscreet? I snapped off the safety on the gun and slowly walked into the room. Somehow it felt okay. And it was, an electrician in work clothes was in the room changing light bulbs. I gave him a relieved hello and settled in for the night.

It was a long, anxious, surreal night. I tried to set up the room as a fortress. I moved the furniture around, put the TV in front of me on the couch I laid on and laughably (later) put pots and pans on the floor in front of the door in case I fell asleep so I would hear someone enter. I turned off all the lights except for the light from the bathroom door next to the entrance so I could see clearly and get a shot or two off. The whole situation seemed unreal, and I accused myself of melodrama. For most of the night I waited, laying on the couch, facing the door but toward dawn, tired and less frightened, I even slept for an hour. I resolved to call Anderson first thing in the morning on his beeper.

I had coffee before I called Anderson. "They found out about me" I said, "they broke into my storage unit" I heard him take a deep breath. "I'll set you up with an appointment to see an agent there." "An appointment?" Yes, he said, and in the interim 911 would be my best bet for protection. I hung up. 911. I was on my own. So much for government concern or protection. I paced the room a while thinking about how I would react if they confronted me, something I fully expected. It was after nine now and I needed to work. I never thought seriously about <u>not</u> going in. Finally, I decided if they challenged me I would tell them to go to hell that I was in the arms of the Feds. I finished my second cup of coffee and went downstairs.

And there he was in the lobby talking to the desk clerk, the guy I had seen at the storage unit and who had broken into my locker. It stunned me. They had set him up in the same hotel and that's how he knew when I was leaving for the International and then storage unit. I went back upstairs and got the pistol. I wasn't sure what I was doing. My concern was what he might intend to do with me. I went downstairs carrying my briefcase in my left hand and the pistol in my right hand in my jacket pocket. He no longer was in the lobby. I walked outside and saw him waiting outside. A flash of recognition crossed his face, and he frowned.

I walked past him into the street and then purposely turned toward an underpass and a deserted part of the street. I gripped the gun. If he was out to harm me, I wanted him to make his move while I was ready and could defend myself. As I walked to the underpass, I decided I would shoot him if he followed me, no questions asked. I was surprised at my ruthlessness but if I hesitated at all, I would be the one dead. I stopped and waited in the underpass. He did not follow. I walked back up on the other side the street. He was sitting now with a small piece of baggage by his side. He was waiting for a bus to take him to the airport, likely back to Chicago. They had hired him to do a job, and he had done it well. I still wonder if I would have hesitated in that underpass.

Everybody knew. I could tell that from the way people looked at me. Grogan came in talking loudly to nobody in particular, (which was his normal entrance). He saw me going into my cubicle. "A Socialist" he said out loud, "a Socialist" he repeated. The "Socialism" comment came from the tapes; that was the only way he could have known that about my former connection with Socialist groups in Chicago; I had never discussed these experiences with anyone at the International because it was something I had learned to treat with discretion. Now I knew for sure he had heard the tapes.

I went to my cubicle and started cleaning out some of my personal things from my desk. I figured I wouldn't have too much time to do this later. I was busy doing this when I looked up and saw Leavitt standing in the cubicle's door. "How you doing" his face was impassive. I nodded, "okay". He looked at me. "How's the back?". "Better," I said. "That's good" he said, he started to leave then stopped and turned around, "We don't know what to do with you" he said flatly and left. It was one of those surprising moments of candor that I had experienced several times with Leavitt during my time at the union. I took a deep breath. I sensed I would be all right, at least for a while. I put my stuff back into the desk.

My time at the International was short, so I redoubled my efforts. At lunch, I started making calls to public interest groups from a payphone in a nearby hotel. I decided I wanted to start a civil Racketeer Influenced and Corrupt Organizations (RICO) suit against the union officers by myself and some members if I could find any willing to do so. I needed help. I called GAP, (Governmental Accountability project); CPAs for the Public Interest, the ACLU and the litigation group from Ralph Nader's public Interest group. None offered help. "They didn't do union stuff." I began to feel like a crank or a fanatic running around D.C. telling a story no one was interested in hearing. I began doubting myself again.

I tried to get media attention focused on the union. I wrote "60 Minutes", "20/20" and "Frontline" telling them about the abuses in the union and the failure of the DOL and the accounting firm and the organized crime element. Only "Frontline" expressed an interest. One staff member seemed keenly interested. "We have done nothing on labor for a while" he said. I sent them a lot of data to support my claims. They looked hard at it but decided that some other programs had a higher news value and priority. "Maybe later" the staff person said.

The doubts started again: Could all this financial stuff just normal behavior? Was I naïve or simple? Didn't the government have financial abuses, corruption? And what about corporations? Maybe this was commonplace, acceptable, and I wasn't sophisticated enough to understand the facts of life. I talked again that week with Art Fox. I told him what was going on. He thought it was as wrong as I did and that was reinforcing. He asked the obvious, "Are you concerned about your safety". "Somewhat," I said. The 1991 HEREIU general convention was coming up, and I wanted to send a letter to all the delegates telling them what was going on at the International. It would be my parting shot. Fox wasn't enthusiastic. "Why don't you just immolate yourself in front of the convention?" was his sarcastic response.

His comment triggered an association in my mind. Martyrdom has long been an ideal in Catholicism and the Church has a long list of martyrs. Martyrdom makes one a potential candidate for sainthood. My baptismal name had been Sebastian after Saint Sebastian, a Roman soldier who had been shot full of arrows by the Romans after refusing to renounce his conversion. The church had a marble statute of him, (filled with arrows in his torso his eyes cast upward toward heaven) in the altar's front. I remember kneeling in the church staring reverently for long times at the white marble statue envying a man who was still admired two thousand years after his death. I realized that ideal still had some strange and dangerous magnetism for me. I junked the idea of a letter.

Later that week, I kept the appointment Anderson made for me with a local IRS organized crime agent. It was a waste of time. Anderson still suspicious of my motives, had briefed him with the idea that I was one of the boys who had been discovered snitching and was now running scared. The agent said, "Okay, so Anderson has been giving you money to inform right?" It offended me. I had never asked for or taken a dime. I was doing this out of idealism and this guy, the agent, was the one getting paid to do what he was doing. He was effectively the mercenary, not me. After some talk, the agent realized I was for real and he turned sympathetic advising me to get help from public interest organizations. I didn't bother to tell him I had already done that.

I also talked with the FBI by phone that week but the agent at first didn't believe me. "Why would they just take your tapes and not make it look like a burglary? We talked a while, and he said he would check with his supervisor. When I called him back a day later he said, "These are some very tough people but we'll take them on, come in and we'll talk about it". There was something in the agent's voice, an immaturity, a bravado, a studied casualness that put me off. I thought the hell with it; I have had enough of so-called law enforcement. In retrospect this may have been a mistake, but that was my mood then. I realize now or the first time as I write this they could have provided me with some additional protection. It's easy to miss important moves in the turmoil of things.

The next week, I debated strategy in my mind. Someone left a note scrawled with obscenities on my desk, but that didn't disturb me much, it seemed like a spontaneous stupid thing someone had done on their own. I still can't figure out who did it; the handwriting was poor, almost illiterate or perhaps an effort made to disguise it. And a rumor was circulating I was a pervert. They had to discredit me.

One lunchtime I was walking up "M" street toward Wisconsin Avenue in Georgetown when a large gray auto came up quickly alongside me and slammed on the brakes hard. I turned around and recognized an officer from a west coast local at the wheel. He was a sergeant-at-arms at the conventions, a strongman monitor. Rumor had it he was a former pro football player. Right now he was playing at intimidation. However, I wasn't intimidated. I merely looked at him like he was crazy and continued my walk up the street. They were bluffing with this stuff and I knew it.

In fact, the bluffing somewhat reassured me because they knew I was working with the government and that if anything happened to me they thought it would be big trouble for them. They didn't want to bring the government down on the union. And I also realized that any real serious threat to my well-being would come from the organized crime types outside the union not from within the union itself. My concern now was not that somebody in power might order any retaliation on me but that someone might act ad hoc and do so. Somebody who wanted to ingratiate themselves with the higher-ups.

I have to admit to momentarily feeling as if I betrayed the people at the union. It was a transitory one that I got past quickly by remembering it was they who betrayed the members not me. However, this illustrates how deeply the cultural concept of loyalty can be. Even though I had deliberately kept a distance between myself and the other personnel and I knew deep down I was doing the right thing I still experienced a sense of disloyalty.

I realized that the tension caused by my discovery was significant and wouldn't diminish. I also had to be concerned about my safety. I offered them my resignation, and they acknowledged it immediately with a certified letter requiring my signature. I had solved their problem of what to do with me. Since I felt somewhat secure, I left the actual date open. They sent me to Atlantic City where the Feds were already in under the theory I couldn't do any harm there.

I went to Atlantic City the former domain of Nicodemus, (Little Nicky) Scarfo, a ruthless and wanton killer, who even killed relatives of his enemies, a vendetta the Mafia did not normally do He received a monthly bag of money from the Atlantic City local from Frank Gerace, an Atlantic City local official and a trustee on the International Welfare Funds. They named Gerace in Senate testimony as a Scarfo associate. Some officers, Al Diadone, and Ray "Long John" Martorano, a Scarfo associate, convicted of killing a union competitor, John McCullough by sending a hit-man to his home with a flower delivery during the Christmas holidays. (The most creative killing I've read about was a guy dressed in a costume on Halloween who whacked a guy.) Another officer, Ralph Natale, was sentenced to 30 years for narcotics trafficking and other offenses.

It was reported that the union through its officers funneled $125,000 in cash to the then Atlantic City mayor Michael Matthews to help Scarfo get city real estate property he wanted. They convicted Scarfo of multiple counts in 1988 and died in prison in January 2017. His son, Nick Jr., a Lucchese family soldier, was sentenced to 30 years in prison. Like father, like son. They removed Frank Gerace as an officer of the local and wound up as a paid consultant at $48,000 a year. Later when the government removed him from this job, he landed on his feet with a position at the International. The crooks take care of their own.

Atlantic City was a local permeated with organized crime influence, and the DOL and FBI went into the local and the government took it over under a trusteeship. The Justice Department filed a racketeering suit and barred Ed Hanley from any contact, even communicating with the local during the trusteeship of the local. Listed as a defendant the Justice Department RICO suit said: "Hanley was an associate of senior members of the Chicago-based family of La Cosa Nostra ("LCN") and involved with New York and Philadelphia LCN members." Hanley agreed to the ban, resulting in the rather bizarre situation of an International president not even being able to talk with his local.

I remember being at the International when the government first took over the local. I overheard a call from Hanley's secretary to the International's legislative section, asking them for a record of political contributions to New Jersey politicos. A hired gun public relations man went to work smoothing the situation over, explaining in press releases that Hanley had accepted the Justice Department communications ban to avoid litigation expense for the union. Yeah, like he gave a damn about expenses of the union.

The International had its own lobbyist a guy who I heard rumored was once a personnel man at the Hilton Hotel in Chicago before Hanley selected him to be the man on the Hill for the union paying him $250,000 a year for his efforts. He had an office at the International and another one in D.C. where he handled other clients. HEREIU considered him good at what he did on the Hill but he didn't impress me after I heard him one morning telling "queer" jokes to a small group of Capital hill types including a congressman. Hanley through his relationship with Rostenkowski and other politicians to was able to prevent important tax legislation that would have been detrimental to the union.

John Wilhelm

Atlantic City had that tough quality of urban unions. Two trouble-shooters from the International came down to help with the transition of the local through the government trusteeship. The two men were formerly of the New Haven local who along with John Wilhelm formed a group I dubbed the "New Haven boys". They were the so-called progressives of the union. They had won a big victory in New Haven organizing the housekeeping employees at Yale University after a long bitter fight. It is always a puzzle to me that huge endowed non-profits, in education and healthcare organizations that are constantly declaring their compassion for people, fight so desperately to deprive their lower-level employees of a decent living wage.

Wage theft is an ignored national scandal costing vulnerable, low-income workers and estimated by the Economic Policy Institute at 15 billion dollars a year. This also includes white-collar workers who are misclassified as management to avoid time and a half wages. Although the Fair Labor Standards Act specifically prohibits wage theft. The Institute found that the percentage of enforcement was 0.01%. State enforcement is just as poor. The NC DOL is an classic example of that failure to protect workers safety and wages. The national DOL had 1000 investigators for 7.3 million workplaces. Congress and the DOL are failing workers again. Despite this, the Good Jobs First organization in June 2018 reported that federal and state wage theft cases of 4002 resulted in 9.2 billion in penalties. Another 8.8 billion assessed on 1200 cases against corporations. Walmart alone had 1.4 billion in penalties. They could assess much more, the problem is just that pervasive in small workplaces as well as large ones.

Early on, I was very enthusiastic about the New Haven boys, thinking they would be the vanguard of a clean union whenever that opportunity might happen. They were my hope for the future of the union once Hanley left. However, as time passed, they began to draw large salaries and perks; I had the sense they were getting very comfortable with "Edward" as they advanced through the union. The Atlantic City government monitor also seemed charmed by Hanley and told me a story of how he played golf with him and found Hanley had a great sense of humor. The monitor wound up as a trustee on the union's welfare funds.

In fairness, I think it is possible Hanley had some vision about the union and wanted to establish one with young straight shooting blood. The government looked at it as a "cover" for Hanley and the Mob and they are probably right, but I give him the skeptical benefit of the doubt. Hanley I believe had two sides to his personality: the Irish Catholic one with its imprinted conscience and subsequent guilt and the crooked side, out for himself and willing to do anything with anybody to get what he wanted. It is completely clear, however, he had no regard for the dues of hundreds of thousands of his hardworking, low-income members and used their money like it was his for his benefit so that argues for the government's opinion.

The FBI was at the local as was Chance from the DOL Racketeering Section. They were weeding out Mob connected business agents and employees. It was out and out funny, a big FBI agent with a blue baseball hat, whom I hadn't met, was standing talking to a female clerk when I walked up to them. "Are you undercover" she asked him. "Yes, I am", he said solemnly. I was tempted to tell him he just blew his cover, but I didn't want to spoil his dramatics so I let it go. The monitor, a small, rotund man with a bulldog like demeanor, was on the phone when I came into his office. When he hung up, I asked him if he had checked the phone system for taps. "No," he said. "We probably should have." Although he was walking into a den of thieves, he didn't even do the basics. That's the way life is.

A computer scam at the local siphoned off local funds. The union had given a lucrative computer contract to a man who was fighting the monitor's efforts to remove him without compensation. I was there to put in a new computer system so I had to talk to him about the lack of cooperation. "I don't have any problem with you guys" he said when I confronted him about getting some information for the new computer that he had refused to give the monitor. I got the information. He didn't give up his scam without a fight and later sued the local union which I understand he lost. Guys like him develop a twisted sense of morality that finds them outraged if you stop them from stealing like it entitles them to the thefts.

Coming from Chicago and having been around the block in terms of exposure to some bad environments, it is easy to recognize one and Atlantic City qualified. Some people were the kind that considered corruption as natural as breathing. They accepted characteristics in their co-workers that many of us would find objectionable. One guy, "Ace", a man in his late fifties who treated members like dirt, used to steal from lunches in the refrigerator. Everybody knew he did it. When I asked the janitor why people accepted that ugly habit, his response was matter-of-fact, "That's just Ace," he said.

There was a female accountant who was cooperating with the FBI. She was worried about retaliation. At one point, she stayed home for days from work pondering whether to continue to cooperate with the government. I was standing next to here when another female employee whose relatives had been removed by the government came up to her and said, "What goes around comes around." The accountant turned to me and said, "I think I've just been threatened.",Ultimately she continued to cooperative with the government.

It startled me to learn that there was a psychologist at the union, an attractive blond woman who was part of a program to help union members with substance abuse problems. We used to have coffee at the same time and started to talk by Mr. Coffee brewer. One of her clients was the president of the union who said to be on coke. "My colleagues call me the Margaret Mead of the Mafia, " she told me. I laughed. I liked her. She was smart and personable.

I forget the context of the conversation, but at one point she alluded to having a "secret". We made a date for dinner to talk about her secret, which she promised to share with me. We went for dinner in a comfortable restaurant with a bar. We picked up the menus, "what would you like to drink" I asked. "I'm a recovering alcoholic," she said, matter-of-factly, "but it doesn't bother me if you drink" I skipped it. Half-way through a pleasant dinner, she started to share her story with me. She was from out west and had been into drugs herself and her boyfriend had been murdered.

"Not by me" she added quickly. She had gone through addiction and alcoholism treatment and was now clean for years. But that wasn't the secret. The secret was that she was part of a small select group chosen by God and led by a male guru who would be the present at the Second Coming which was to take place at the New Millennium. I was stunned, speechless. This charming, intelligent woman was telling me something that in some circumstances would be considered psychotic. "You're spooking me," I said. "I know," she said. I took her home to her hovel as she called it.

It was just that, a tiny half basement with an entrance under a stairway. In her bedroom was a picture of her bearded guru, flanked by candles on a little altar covered with a red cloth. She had gone from drugs to fantasy to keep herself going. I kissed her good night and left. I am still stunned and touched by her story and I've wondered. What she did when nothing happened in the Year 2000. Her cult leader probably changed the date of the apocalypse. When I left the local, I told the Latino guy to monitor and help her if she needed it.

The government cleaned up the union. I put the local's books on computer and produced financial statements that I insisted be given to the members at the next union meeting. I had to fight for it, the New Haven boys thought it was too much information and the monitor needed to be convinced. The members got the statements and had a great time asking questions at the meeting. They hit on everything from the trivial to the important and I could see the New Haven boys squirming under the interrogation. I felt good about setting the precedent. My view is that the money is the membership's and they have every right to know about every penny that is spent by the union.

Curiously, some International staff's reactions to my discovery, while unspoken, were sympathetic. It puzzled me at first and then I understood that the psychiatrist's tapes had also described some of my childhood and my current loneliness. I have to admit I liked that sensitivity. They were human despite our differences. Thinking about the tapes, I also had a good laugh. There were those times during which, as I mentioned, just for fun and perhaps out of loneliness, I had spirited conversations (rather one-sided) with Wolfgang. I would tell Wolfgang about this or that, ask him what he thought about it, laugh and just carry on as if he were a silent partner.

I could visualize the listeners to the tape wondering, worrying about who the fuck Wolfgang was and how he was involved in all of this. Unfortunately, the tapes had repercussions for my Nigerian programmer. The tape of the federal agents discussing putting an agent in the International made the listeners wonder if the Nigerian was the plant that was discussed, (they had no way of dating the tape) and he was dismissed after I left. I felt bad about this but there was nothing I could do about it. I know his dismissal puzzled him. He landed on his feet with a job with a government agency.

I met Hanley the following week on the street one evening as I was returning to the International after a goodbye dinner with one employee, a secretary who had taken care of my union affairs while I was on the road. She introduced me to him although he recognized who I was. I saw fear cross his face. The secretary was oblivious to the situation, "His parents came from the same part of Ireland your ancestors came from," she said, smiling. Hanley was quickly extraditing himself from the encounter, "beautiful country," he said, as he hurried away. The secretary they pressured into early retirement because of her friendly relationship with me although she was close to it anyhow.

Hanley's grandparents came from El Fin in County Roscommon. a short distance from where my mother was born and I had heard her talk of it. My grandfather was from that area, but his name was Hanily. In a trip to Ireland in 1975, I had found a tombstone dated 1642 with the name Hanily on it. I wondered if it were possible we may have been related at some ancestral stage; that would have had added an interesting touch of irony to the whole affair. I saw Hanley again, the next day, as he entered the elevator at the International. I was walking past him toward the lobby. "How you doing?" I said. "All right" he said, but his face flushed with anger.

My RICO suit received no support. I contacted an attorney with a reputation as concerned with labor issues. He was a very well paid legal counsel for a professional sports organization. I sent him a FedEx package and called on it afterwards. He promised to look at it. I could tell from his voice he wasn't interested. Six weeks later his secretary told me it was still laying on his desk unopened. It annoyed me, "Tell him he's doing me and my cause a disservice" I said. He refused to talk to me on the phone after that. And this was a guy who spoke at the AUD convention on fighting labor corruption. Some guys are big on talk at conventions but small on action in their lives unless they are well paid for it.

I wrote a three-page letter to a few attorneys detailing my case for a RICO which in reviewing it years later still makes sense but there were no takers. I wrote David Reich then Secretary of Labor (who despite his deep concern on social justice issues to this day did little to improve his Department of Labor during his tenure). I told him of my disappointment over the lack of direct elections and the short time of the monitor-ship. I got a response from the Inspector General, Charles Masten, who essentially in bureaucratize legalese blew it off saying that "while it was true the consent decree didn't call for direct elections it provides for the Review Board's approval of candidates". This is the IG's rather limited view of democracy in action. You know what happens when the Review Board leaves in a year or so. The wise watchdog Association of Union Democracy saw it coming with a headline at the start of the monitor-ship, "Bold Beginning but watch the endgame." At the end, the headline was "What's new in the Hotel monitor-ship? Nothing!" They cited the lame results and the lack of direct elections along with not informing members of news on the monitor-ship.

I still had some time left at the International. Now that I had assured them I was leaving, I was taking my time in doing so. I wanted to go shopping, one more time. I waited until everyone went to the convention, (I checked the airline billing manifesto and their reservations name by name to be sure) and then I made one more extensive shopping trip. The International was deserted except for two clerks on the first floor who were answering the phones. This time I pulled out the stops and worked for everything. I booted the IBM computer and printed out every transaction in and out of the union for the past five years. It took two reams of paper and 15 hours to run off. I carted off two boxes of printouts and put them in my trunk. Later I turned over all this information to the DOL with the stipulation that I could have it back if I ever wanted it. One box contained 20 items representing, propositions, expense reports of Hanley, credit card bills, correspondent, financials, pension fund statements, phone accounts, records of the motor home, payroll ledgers, etc. It was my final dump.

I flew to the convention midweek. I had to demonstrate an accounting program. I was nervous going to Chicago. Now that the word was out on me I didn't know what to expect. If something is going to happen to somebody, it will happen in Chicago. Instead of staying at the convention hotel with everyone else I booked a room at the Drake, a hotel by the Oak Street Beach and a mile from the Palmer House where the convention was being held. My mother worked at the Drake as a maid when we were on Clark Street. If anyone ever doubts we have a class system in America all they need to do is look at the plush ambiance of hotels like the Drake. Then walk back through the door marked "employees" and see the grim faded green rooms and hallways where the employees walk, the stark rooms where take their breaks and have lunch.

I attended one event at the 1991 convention, an accounting demonstration of a software package I had selected to do the local's financials. I took part in a discussion on the package afterward, making some suggestions on its implementation. I did well under a tremendous amount of pressure. As soon as it was over I left. I said hello to Massey in the elevator on the way out. He said nothing. Afterwards I walked over to State Street and listened to some street blues then back to the Drake to check out.

My union days were over.

CHAPTER TEN:
MY UNION DAYS ARE OVER

The greater the risk, the sweeter the fruit
- Pierre Corneille

I was too young to retire, but I knew that I was dead in the labor movement, so I made no effort to find work right away. Fox tried to talk me into a job with the Postal Employee's Union, one of his clients, so I could help some new officers keep straight on their financial dealings. By then I had enough of union officials and their financial styles and I passed on the offer. "You can't retire," he said. "You've got to do this." I shook my head. "No way, it's a thankless job." "You'll never get another job in a labor union after your experience at the International" he said. But I didn't care. I wasn't about to follow around some careless officers spending union money illegal or not. I didn't feel like being a watchdog. I had enough.

But I didn't know what to do with myself or where to go. I feared going back to Chicago. I visited my brother in Atlanta, Georgia, where my mother was now. When I first went to Atlanta, my niece answered a phone call and gave the phone to me. "It's for you, she said". I took it and there was no response and then a click. I knew they knew where I was. This will sound like an odd interpretation but I felt they were calling to see if I was okay, that Grogan felt some guilt at causing my departure. They heard the therapy tapes and just wanted to know I landed on my feet.

But I couldn't rely on that feeling, so I took my brother's gun to a shooting range and practiced.

My mother became ill while I was down there. She stopped eating. We took shifts, myself and my sister-in-law. I would lie on a cot on the floor next to her bed all night and she would watch her during the day. We did that for months. It appeared she would die. A nurse would come in periodically. I vividly remember one night how she raised her hands toward the ceiling calling out the names of her sisters who she saw there, talking with them. It was a dramatic scene; I was sure she was ready to die, but I talked with an Italian doctor who gave me hope and sure enough under his care she improved. I was fortunate to find a good nursing home on a tip and she moved over there and lived comfortably three more years. My brother visited her daily.

My older sister died during that time, lung cancer. She was ill for a few months in Chicago. During that time I never visited her and when I finally did it, she died on the weekend I was going up there. I'll never understand why I waited. She was the one relative that meant something to me and who loved me and I left her to die without seeing her. I can't forgive myself for that unforgivable neglect and it haunts me. I feel sick every time I think of it and I deserve every moment of that feeling.

I left Atlanta then and roamed the country again: Louisville, Austin, Dallas, the mountains of North Carolina staying for a few months in each place. I kept searching for a permanent place to live in but I couldn't seem to settle down. I don't know of that was fear of discovery or that I couldn't stop the travel habit. Maybe both.

In Asheville, I met a Myra in the botanical garden who was a Catholic peace activist. She was part of the Catholic underground, folks who laid in front of military trains and demonstrated against facilities who trained paramilitaries for Central America. Myra was a small plain woman with a worn demeanor. She envisioned herself a kind of "Mother Teresa". Myra had no ongoing relationship with a man but told me she met with someone she had a relationship once a year for sex and renewed friendship. Kind of reminded me of the book/film "Same Time, Next Year".

We had dinner one evening and afterwards went to her apartment. I had never talked about my adventures in the union and after all those years I had this pent-up need to talk to it about somehow to somebody. I thought she would be receptive given her background. So I started talking.

She sat in a couch across from my chair. About five minutes into my story I saw her nodding off then her eyes reopened for a moment, "Yes, she murmured you're an unsung hero" and then she fell soundly asleep. That was the end of my story.

My mother died in January 1994 and I had her body shipped to Chicago. She had picked the plot with me in a Catholic cemetery in 1984; she had liked it because a nice-looking tree shaded it. The visitation had relatives and friends and a sudden surprise when Grogan showed up. It is traditional in unions to have a union representative show at the funeral of members but this was an ad hoc appearance by him since I was now out of the union. He knelt at the casket and then came over to me and shook hands. "How you doing Hughie?" "Okay" I said warily, wondering what the hell he wanted. "Where are you living now": I ignored the question.

He had been in Chicago and seen the obituary in the paper; some Irish read the obits, (dubbed the Irish sporting pages), as a daily habit. On the way out he asked me again, "Where you living now, Hughie?" I gave him the same blank look and silence. However, my real sense of his visit was that he was doing something he thought charitable and was not trying to do me harm. He was just interested in where and what I was doing. He may even have been kind of concerned about me since about in an odd way I believed that Grogan kind of liked and respected me and I sort of appreciated the human gesture of his coming to the visitation.

It was dead winter in Chicago and the city covered in cold snow. We were on our way to a funeral mass at a neighborhood church when we turned north on Ashland Avenue where the hearse was blocked by a truck stuck in the ice and snow. The funeral director had the driver turn it around and we went over to the next accessible block, Clark Street. It took me a few blocks to realize it but when I did a thrill ran through me. *Our funeral procession was going to pass down Clark Street right pass the spot where the six flat had been located. It seemed to me a beautiful accident of fate, (one that she would have appreciated), and a gesture of closure to her life and ours together that we would go right by the place where we had lived and struggled so hard to survive).* It was a moment I will never forget.

The deep freeze weather prevented a graveside service. We had a brief memorial in the cemetery building. On my way out I decided I would try to find the grave. I got directions from the office but once out in the falling snow I couldn't even find the section markers. I wandered around in the snow and stepped into an open grave half covered with board slats that broke my fall on a board and I got up okay. Two gravediggers came by in a vehicle and I asked them where the section was. They knew the grave since they had just worked on it and directed me to it. It was there under the ice-covered tree and I saw my niece had sent some flowers that had been laid down on top of the grave when the casket was put into the ground. Next time I go to Chicago I think I'll pay a visit to make sure it is okay.

I kept in touch with Ron Chance. He had told me in 1991 that a RICO action against the International was being considered. I would call him every so often to see if there were any developments. He would call me for a piece of information. One time he told me the Atlantic City local had free elections for the first time in years. One September morning in 1995 he called: "The DOJ just filed a RICO on the HERE" "You're kidding?" No, they're putting in a court-appointed monitor." We talked for a while about the details. The government was finally acting. I was jubilant. For the first time I felt there would be some real justice for the International.

The government in its initial RICO action charged the General Executive Board with fifteen counts including conspiring with organized crime associates to commit extortion, impinge the rights of members through actual and threatened force, failure to provide representation of the members, failure to enforce the HEREIU constitution, failure to investigate and redress corruption, embezzlement of funds and other assets for personal use, and kickbacks from employers. The RICO action further charged that "for over 25 years, various members and associates of organized crime groups have exercised influence over the HEREIU and various constituent entities". These groups included organized crime groups in New York, Philadelphia, Milwaukee, and Chicago.

I wrote the Monitor, Kurt Mullenberg, a man with an impressive resume as Chief of the Justice Department's organized crime division. It was a 16 page letter telling him everything I could think of that might be helpful in his investigation of the union's activities. It detailed the financial abuses and accounting problems I found and criticized the accounting firm and the DOL. I wrote him of my beliefs and impressions of the personnel at the International and the locals and included my convention letter.

Kurt Muellenberg

I also told him of the bogus local the International had set up in Rhinelander, Wisconsin near the vacation homes of Hanley and some officers. Vice-president O'Gara, Hanley's son Tom and other officers had homes in the area. I had reported this phony local to the DOL back in 1990 but nothing came of it. The local, according to my estimate, had cost the International at least $650,000 during its existence. The government did nothing and didn't seem to care at the time about the phony local like they didn't seem to care about so many other things wrong in the union. I had told the DOL about the $31,000 for "advice on running a union" paid by his son's Local 1 to Hanley. I suspect they passed it on to Mullenberg since he mentions it in his report as "unsolicited material".

The monitor dutifully and importantly removed 23 officials from the various locals for either gangland connections or misuse of union funds. Mullenberg suspended two officials for a year. And Tom Hanley for a year (not enough), fined $25,000 and resigned as Director of Organizing. A number of other "quick" retirements happened. Two consultants, including former Congressman Dan Rostenkowski, recently out of prison for political corruption charges, barred for 13 years. Leavitt, VP John O.Gara and Ed Hanley all charged with manipulating auto leases by paying inflated payments early in the lease to purchase the vehicles at bargain amounts at the end of the leases. Leavitt and Hanley made restitution. O'Gara had since died. Leavitt realizing the game was over, resigned.

The monitor recommended the closing of the International regional offices when he found that the employees there could offer no justification for the office's existence (or their own). Finding that the luxury D.C. condo was an expensive white elephant used only a few times each year he recommended its disposal. The monitor characterized giving per diem and credit cards to retired personnel as "incomprehensible". He found, what I had discovered, that the officers like to play the role of big-time tips with union money often paying more as a tip than the bill itself. Some examples the monitor gave was an $80 tip for a $5.80 bill (probably a nice-looking waitress); another for $100 on a $98.80 bill; and $150 on a $116.45 bill. Many other recommendations relative to improving or instituting basic accounting and financial controls initiated. However, there was nothing about direct elections of officers in his reports.

Despite the RICO, the 1996 general convention was going forward. I decided to make a move toward reform and do at the 1996 general convention what I had not done in 1991, write a "white letter" documenting the financial abuses to all the delegates. I knew many of the delegates were bought or intimidated and others ignored the convention knowing it was undemocratic. But I wanted them all to know about the abuses and be responsible for their votes to the membership. The thought of Hanley and company looting the union for another five years disturbed me greatly, and while I had no grandiose expectations in writing the letter I felt a strong need to do it. I hoped it would at least focus attention on the abuses, perhaps touch some consciences and embolden some action.

The letter was 4 pages dense with information and I detailed the abuses with footnotes and sources for each item. I cited Hanley's total compensation of $346,994 in the previous year, (John Sweeney president of the AFL-CIO made $192,500). I showed how Hanley made $173.00 an hour compared to $5.69 for restaurant employees and called him as greedy as any corporate CEO. I gave specific details on the officer's outrageous perks. I called attention to Hanley's gun arrest, his Atlantic city ban, the allegations of Mob connection, his wild spending and also called for his removal from office under the bylaws of the union. I pointed out that the union finances were in disarray because of gross mismanagement and malfeasance. I gave statistical information on the decline in membership.

I even asked the convention delegates to charge Hanley under a section of the HEREIU constitution with "gross disloyalty and conduct unbecoming a member, activities which bring the International under disrepute (the gun incident and Mafia connections); and misappropriation, fraud, and financial malpractice". The delegates did nothing. I hadn't expected they would do anything but the attack on Hanley was a first, no one had dared to challenge him before and certainly not like this. The document was a hell of a lot of work.

I debated whether to sign the paper personally or to present it as a document from "The Committee for HEREIU". The document didn't need my name on it for the International to know who wrote it. I opted for the Committee approach because I had contacted a handful of dissidents, (called the HERETICS) in some big city locals, most notably San Francisco and Vegas. I hoped that the paper would inspire more members to join this group. Real reform could only come from the membership and the union desperately needed a viable dissident group. I worked 36 hours straight the week before the convention sending out the paper to an enormous amount of media outlets via the internet and postal mail. It went it to politicians and labor-related figures. I stopped only for naps and food. For the first time in five years I was involved with the mission again and it felt good. I realized once more I *needed* this cause to put meaning into my life. And there was always Don Quixote always there in the shadows urging me on.

In doing the paper I attempted to get information under the Freedom of Information Act. The DOJ (in one of those ironic touches that the bureaucracy excels in) replied, more than a year later, they would "expedite" any such information, (I never heard from them) The DOL claimed they had nothing but newspaper clippings on the matter. The government often uses the "under investigation" exclusion in refusing information under the Act but they did not even bother to do that. Whether it was it calculated evasion or simple bureaucratic ineptitude, one has to question the sincerity of the government to provide citizens with information under the Freedom of Information Act.

My paper created a stir at the convention but there was disappointingly little press coverage beyond a series of articles for a Bureau of National Affairs publication sent out to a small but influential group of subscribers involved in labor issues. They published brief articles acknowledging the existence of the convention in the Chicago Sun-Times but nothing on the white paper's revelations. I'm not sure if that was because of the indifference of the newspapers or the fact that Hanley always hated the press and often barred them from union events. Despite the cover of a "Committee for HEREIU" signature on my paper, that the International knew who wrote the material, only I would have been able to do that with the inside information in the white paper.

After the convention when I returned home, I became somewhat paranoid, which used to happen when I did something that courted exposure. I began receiving hang up phone calls late in the evening. They seemed to come about the same time every night, ten o'clock, and I was wondering if someone was trying to pinpoint my presence at home. I began to look around when I went out on the street, trying to see if I saw any suspicious cars parked near the house. I found myself looking in my rear-view mirror when I was driving, wondering if anyone was following me. I have an active imagination at times. However, I wasn't really living in fear, just being careful.

I got a caller ID and bought a 12-gauge shotgun and put in under my bed. I understood the shotgun was not protection. If anyone wanted to hit me, they wouldn't give me a chance to use it, but it provided me with a placebo to my sense of vulnerability and helplessness. The shotgun still is in the closet, I oil it once in a while, the weapon will probably never be fired. Law enforcement traced the nightly phone calls for me. They were from a telemarketer selling the local paper using a computer that hung up if there wasn't a person available to make a pitch. It was the early days of robo calls. In a speech to the convention delegates an angry Hanley denounced the letter saying, "the critics that have expressed their criticism to the salary that is earned by the members of the General Executive Board can go to hell."

Delegate acclamation elected Hanley on Monday morning of the convention week. There was no dissent, no one raised a voice on the financial abuses in the white paper. The 300 delegates sold out the membership once again. Frustrated and angry, that week I destroyed almost all the material I had, including most of the material including the two boxes printouts I had recovered from the DOL. I threw piles of paper and reams of printouts into a large trash can for garbage pickup, this same material which had taken me so much time, effort, and risk to accumulate. I thought that was the end of it all. I was symbolically leaving the experience.

My vow to give up on reforming the union didn't last very long. The defiant arrogance of Hanley's "go to hell" convention speech disturbed me. Afterwards, I sat down at my computer and wrote the following email to with angry sarcasm:

"Congratulations Eddie on another hard fought, democratic convention victory. It was inspiring indeed to see you up there ranting and raving about the glories of your administration to all your paid stooges. We appreciated giving us so much of your time; we could have hardly asked for more. It was very gratifying to get so much attention from the great man himself. The press liked it too, and we expect more quotes from the eloquent "and they can all go to hell" speech. The words, like William Jennings Bryan's Cross of Gold speech, will ring forever in the ears of freedom-loving, democratic trade unionists forever. The sheer power and originality of that cry; Its heart felt sincerity and sophistication would move Anthony "Big Tuna" Accardo to tears."

"Yes, Edward we sat there hanging onto every well-turned phrase marveling at the spirited discussion and debate as the delegates boldly fought for their member's interests and rights. Its men and women like these that made this union what it is today. Nothing. Best of luck, Edward. Don't worry about a thing. When you're out of office, (which may be sooner than you think) just remember your old job as a bartender in Cicero is still open (but please pay your dues). Yes, we know they are high and the per capitas out of sight but you know how it is Eddie, times being what they are, we gotta take care of our officers and delegates. See you on the picket lines Eddie."

I signed it "From the members who already lived in Hell for 25 years."

PS "Incidentally, Edward, considering your days and ways you have a much better chance of going to Hell than we do and we wish you God Speed. Not to worry, you'll have plenty of old friends down there: delegates, vice-presidents, executive board members, Mob associates. You might even think of forming a union."

I emailed via an internet re-mailer so it couldn't be traced back to its source. I admit it was somewhat sophomoric but I couldn't resist the temptation and it was a catharsis. I don't know if he ever read it., I doubt it. Later I learned that the International had promised spending reforms, had frozen in creases in per capita dues and officer salaries. My white paper had some impact after all but I also understood that these "reforms" were cosmetic, political gestures made under pressure, not a real reform.

The big news came later by another phone call from Ron Chance. They had forced Ed Hanley into resignation. He resigned before an Executive Board meeting in Chicago on May 18, 1998 naming John Wilhelm as his successor. The monitor acting on my tip had investigated the Rhineland local. The local never met the legal requirements of a viable local and added no new members over three years. The local's trustee had no union experience, received $48,000 a year, was rarely seen at the office and did landscaping for the union president. It was, as I suspected, a farce. Hanley had closed the local when the monitor came in. The fraudulent local was the big-ticket item that the government used to get Hanley to resign on July 31, 1998.

The Justice Department cut a secret deal granting Hanley immunity from prosecution (the Chicago Sun-Times ran an editorial headline, "Hanley Deal Reeks") and called for a Congressional investigation. Justice refused to comment on the deal or release any information to the House Committee requesting it. They also rejected a Freedom of Information Request by the paper.

Hanley confronted with a choice between resignation and prosecution chose the former and resigned. He retired without having to acknowledge making any "improper expenditures" according to the agreement. He paid a pittance $13,944 on cheating on a leased car. Here is a man that robbed union member out of millions of dollars over decades for his benefit and friends, retires on a $275,000 pension and leaves untouched, (that bothered me!) It impressed Chance that the monitor's results had followed the information in my letter so closely (although his staff had found other things as well). The paper bullet had found its mark and my whistle finally heard.

But not loud enough. There was more work to do. While his departure from the union was very important since it broke that connection with the Mob. I had wanted to see Hanley prosecuted and, at least a substantial amount of the funds he had used to build an opulent lifestyle, returned to the membership. Politics was again interfering with justice. Mullenberg would later say he knew nothing about the deal, a curious comment from a man who was intimately involved in the union's affairs including the findings that led to the resignation and even signed the agreement, (without reading it?)

The HEREIU monitor-ship continued on for a year and a half and then extended another year. This brief period was wholly inadequate to the task of rooting out a culture of corruption that had existed for 25 years. I believe it reflected the government's lack of real political will to thoroughly reform the union. The incomplete results of the intervention demonstrated this failure.

The monitor's report highlighted the fact that the union "suffered from a management deficit" and "did not subscribe to generally accepted accounting principles" and that there was a "clear disregard to cost-effective management" (three classic understatements). Despite these charges, he never took either the DOL audit group or the certified accountants to task for their failure to report on the financial abuses that continued for 25 years in the union. Mullenberg didn't want to go there.

Although LMDRA holds Executive Board members liable to the membership for violations of their fiduciary duties. Mullenberg made no attempt to recover any of the tens of millions of dollars funneled from the union over the years by the officers and others from them or the perpetrators.

Instead Mullenberg settled for a gesture, the recovery of paltry $29,000 from Hanley and Leavitt for manipulating car lease payments so they could buy the cars at a bargain price at the end of the lease. Mullenberg's investigation included a review of 837 financial propositions over a 15-month period. He found that 99.5% of the props approved unanimously. He did not, however, remove the executive board for its complicity in the union's financial abuses. I say silence is assent in this case.

Despite the Justice Department's widely publicized proclamations to return "This captive union to democracy," the monitor did not try to implement direct elections of officers (as done in the Teamster and Laborer interventions). The members remained precluded from any direct voice in selecting their leadership, leaving that choice in the hands of controlled delegates who had historically proved their lack of independence from the International leadership. This particular lapse of the intervention was deeply disturbing to me since I viewed direct elections as the one democratic safeguard the members had to remove corrupt officers. The monitor collected over $300,000 a year for his mediocre efforts. The government seems as adept at the Mob is milking the member's dues. Why can't government employees with extensive union and racketeering experience do these monitor-ships at a fraction of the exorbitant and prohibitive costs.

James Jacobs, a very respected academic who has followed union corruption for decades wrote in one of the best books on the subject in "Mobsters, Unions, and Feds. He states "Although some of HEREIU's most notorious members were expelled and they forced Hanley to resign Mullenberg's investigations and disciplinary actions not nearly as extensive as those of the independent administrator and Independent Revew Board in the Teamster case. Mullenberg focused surprisingly little attention on identifying or purging organized crime's influence from the union. He also did not make it a top priority to investigate and remedy racketeering in HEREIU locals. No change as made in HEREIU's election procedures." (delegate elections of officers rather than a member elected ones).

Mullenberg's monitor-ship raises questions about his competence or seriousness in doing his job. His efforts seemed to go through the motions. My conversation with him was curious; he struck me as a sort of *bon vivant* with a cavalier attitude toward it all. He referred to Leavitt as a "likable rogue". In another interview with the press he referred to the union's nepotism and political clout as "a Chicago thing." Describing Hanley's largesse with his friends Mullenberg said, "If I were down and out and I needed some help, I would be lucky to have a friend like Mr. Hanley." (Hanley was lucky to have a friend like Mullenberg).

Mullenberg established an 800 number for calls from members on corruption problems, (which was ineffective) but resisted efforts to publicize the activities of the monitor-ship to the membership in the monthly newsletter as had occurred in the Teamster intervention. Notifying the membership of the removal of Mob connected officers would have been important in reducing fear in the membership and restoring some trust in their remaining officers. The monitor published a page (the back one) in the HERE bi-monthly news magazine, Catering Industry Employee Nov./Dec/, 1998 in which the front two pages extolled the union's cooperating with the monitor, listed some of his disciplinary action but no mention of Hanley's forced resignation.

That item appears in the back page report of the monitor. He believed the problem with corruption in the locals was because of a "lack of understanding of their fiduciary obligations" and recommended training to improve their sensitivity to such issues as extravagant salaries, bonuses, and separation packages. "Sensitivity", as if they weren't damned aware of what they were doing all the time. The San Francisco Heretics at Local 2 lampooned Muellenberg as the smiling, affable, somewhat silly "Maytag Man" on TV commercials.

It strikes me as remarkably naïve for a man who has spent a lifetime in law enforcement to assume that union officers regardless of lack of education or fiduciary sophistication don't fully realize that the money they are spending for their own benefit is the member's money, not theirs. If they didn't understand this elemental fact, why would they go to such lengths to conceal such spending? Mullenberg, rather than distribute the final report to the membership, gave only one copy to each local, a process which would force a member to go into the local and request to see the report, an act that would automatically put the member at risk in some locals and mark him or her as a potential troublemaker in others. Mullenberg, like some union officers, seemed to have forgotten that he was being paid by the membership not the union officials. Labor Notes a highly respected periodical that reports on unions said in an article published July 9,1998 that the monitor-ship was a "deeply flawed failure"

Wayne Johnson of the Chicago Crime Commission told a Chicago Magazine writer in 1999 had it right: "People are lulled into a false sense of security and these guys go back to their old ways within a matter of years. In two or three years these guys are back in office and everything's fine." It was true then, it's still true. Corruption at the local level will continue to bear watching for the union especially in the big cities.

An enlightening book cleverly titled "Double Crossed" subtitled "The Failure of Organized Crime Control" published in 2017 by Michael Woodiwiss takes issue with the prevailing sense that organized crime is under control in the U.S. and internationally. He makes an intriguing point of how the General Accounting Office, the GAO, the investigative arm of the Congress had issued 19 reports between 1972 and 1989 with the words "Organized Crime" in the title. Strangely, no report since that time has included those terms. The author criticizes the FBI's antiquated take on organized crime and the illusion that has been created that it is no longer a threat to our society. I think he is on to something.

The final "protection" which was particularly offensive to me at the International was the institution of a three person public Review Board whose function was to ensure that all officials would follow the canon of ethics. Included in the board was James Thompson, "Big Jim", the former governor of Illinois, one of those people who is invariably described in hyperbolic praise who had received political contributions from the union and attended its conventions. His wife Jayne had received almost a hundred thousand dollars for legal work for the International, (a fact neatly omitted from the monitor's report who mentioned the work but not the relationship).

Another Board member was an Archbishop from Chicago, whose seminary in the Chicago area, St. Mary's, had received money from the International and whose religious denomination had received huge contributions from the union over the years. Reverend James Kelleher had gone on record as not being aware of any organized crime problems in the union, (apparently the good father didn't read Chicago newspapers in his efforts to be unworldly). The monitor was the third party on the review board. The measures were laughably inadequate and unimaginative. The board started its life as overseer of the union's ethics by grossly violating its own pronouncements that there was not even to be the "appearance of a conflict of interest by union officials.

My despair at this point was pretty complete. The intervention I had hoped for and waited for so many years had failed to do the job of reform: it did not honor the membership by doing justice to the massive fraud that had occurred in the union for 25 years. No prosecutions occurred, (to date I don't believe anyone has served one day in jail, whoever said "Crime Doesn't pay" must have been looking at the wrong racket); it did not install democratic process in the union; and did not implement meaningful preventive measures which would prevent future corruption. The Justice Department "dismissed" the lawsuit against the union early. I realized also the government would not intervene again for at least another generation.

The part-time Public Review Board (PRB) continued with its three members, ostensibly maintaining and promoting ethics in the union and spending eight hundred thousand dollars a year in doing it. The International selected two of the members and will select any future members. This hardly makes for an independent board. I contacted activist members asking them what the PRB is doing and they do not understand since it apparently does not publish its activities. The members continued to be exploited, this time by the "reformers". It is revealing to note that the expenses incurred by unions in reform efforts by the government in RICO_have been extraordinary and so exorbitant in the Teamster's case intervention that they threatened the financial stability of the union itself. It seems like even the government can't keep their fingers out of the union dues cookie jar either.

CHAPTER ELEVEN:
I ASK FOR AN ACCOUNTING

One hour in the execution of justice is worth seventy years of prayer
- Islamic saying

From the beginning, the lack of ethics displayed by the auditors outraged me. It was my belief that they gave the union an aura of legitimacy with their certified audits every year. I was all too aware of the enormous fees that they collected for what I considered collusion in the financial abuses of the union. Accounting ethics would require the firm to withdraw from the audit engagement with the union rather than perpetuate the financial charade played on the members and the public. SAS #54 (Statement on Auditing Standards) concerns itself with illegal acts and requires pro-active action by auditors on any such acts that impact the financial statements materially such as manipulation, falsification, misclassification, or alteration of accounting records or supporting documents or misrepresentation or intentional omission of transactions. The accountants completely ignored this rule. They were as culpable as the corrupt union officers.

I blew the whistle on the firm. I filed a formal complaint with the American Institute of Certified public Accountants, (AICPA), requesting them to investigate and determine whether the firm had violated professional ethics in their relationship with the union. I provided them with the 64 page monitor's report which had cataloged the abuses and criticized the union's incredible lack of accounting controls. Remarkably, and perhaps revealing to note that despite the blatant abuses, the monitor leveled no criticism at the accounting firm in his report.) Enron at least had some sophistication in its accounting fraud, the union, unconcerned with the possibility of any action by the accounting firm or the DOL, was obvious in their greedy games.

There has been a great deal of discussion and litigation as to the responsibility of auditing firms to what are termed "reliant third parties" i.e., those who rely on financial statements for information on an organization's financial integrity. The consensual judicial sense is that while auditors do not have a responsibility to anyone who reads their statements they do indeed have a responsibility to those reliant third parties who hold an economic interest in the financials. And those who rely on them to form an opinion on an organization's financial worth, (in this case union members). They also presume accountants to have an "obligation to the public interest" an obligation that the profession has only paid lip service to in the past.

It occurs to me now that during a 25 year career in accounting which "took me around the block" with work in government, public accounting firms, corporations, and non-profits, I never heard much of "ethics" unless it was in a public scandal and the lack of ethics of some person or group. At lunch we talked about clients, colleagues, sports, politics, TV, occasionally accounting or tax changes, but never ethics. The general sense of ethics was that they were those public relation pronouncements of organizations nice to read and found framed in an executive's office or on the back page of an annual report. In the workplace, accounting street sense, which translated into what the boss of the organization implicitly or explicitly wanted, dictated ethics not the pious proclamations of the profession. During all those years, I never received one memo or letter devoted to ethics nor did I ever attend a meeting on the subject. The subject just never came up. Have things changed? Maybe some due to external pressures, but I doubt if it's enough.

As a young accounting student taking an intermediate accounting course at Northwestern night school, I remember the session before the final exam when the students quizzing the instructor what material to review for the exam. The professor ran through the big text and when he came to Chapter Fifteen, (which he had never assigned), he said, "And Chapter Fifteen you can read it if you want but nothing on it will be in the exam". Chapter Fifteen was the one on professional ethics. Until recently, the CPA exam review, which covers 2300 pages, devoted 30 pages or a mere one percent to ethics. This is from the Internet on the current ethics exam related to the CPA exam:

1. Who administers the CPA Ethics Exam?

While some states run their own ethics exam or courses, most state boards pick the professional Ethics Exam administered by the AICPA.

2. Does every state require a CPA Ethics Exam?

No, only 35 or so state boards require their prospective CPAs to take the ethics exam. Please double check and see if this exam is necessary.

3. Is the CPA Ethics Exam Difficult?

Not really. The exam is more like a self-study, open-book test. However, since the passing score is 90, you need to be careful when reading and selecting the correct answer for the questions.

Make your own judgment.

The AICPA Ethics Committee response was unimpressive. They lost my complaint, and I refilled it. I called to get a time frame on the disposition of my complaint. A weary sounding staff person was apologetic, "I'm sorry", she said, "we have a tremendous backlog and a tiny staff". The AICPA relied on volunteers to staff their Ethics Committee which shows how much emphasis or care they assign to it. They transferred my complaint from one person to another further delaying its processing.

The Ethics Committee told me they would explore whether the facts justified an investigation and if one occurred, they would notify me. Several months later they notified me they continued investigating but that they would not reveal the final results to me, although I was the complainant. However, if there was any serious disciplinary action it would be published in the AICPA newsletter, a publication that goes out only to the membership preventing any public knowledge of the ethical problem in the firm. (Note: the AICPA responding to criticism as the result of the Enron affair is now publishing disciplinary actions by the Ethics Committee).

Individual disciplinary actions are on their website, an improvement over the secrecy of past years. It showed 997 enforcement cases at the beginning of 2018 and 967 at the end of it including 118 deferred because of pending litigation. There were 517 cases opened, 547 closed. 128

expelled. Doesn't seem like much progress in resolving cases. Many suspensions result in corrective action which includes training and education. Suspensions and "Admonishments" are removed from the website after one year when "corrective action" has been taken. (Sort of like removing a malpractice suits on a doctor after a year on a State Medical website) Members who know of "deficiencies" by other members are encouraged to report it, (hopefully competitors :-)

To their credit, the AICPA has done two things: started an extensive Peer Review program wherein the auditors are audited by peers and graded. They loosened up their confidentiality restrictions to allow CPAs to report illegality by clients to outside parties when internal efforts fail. That's a big one. They also maintain a relationship with the DOL to investigate their referrals. They've improved but they are still not there. You don't hold a backlog that big and old if you really care that much about aggressively enforcing ethics in the profession.

Congressional testimony before reform efforts showed that 43% of unions either file their annual reports late or not at all. The DOL (the Department of Laxity or is it Laziness) had no power to enforce filing through civil penalties. They have corrected this with ostensible fines of $100,000 and up to one year in jail for violations. I don't know if they levied these fines against any union. They wouldn't tell me. The antiquated annual report of the DOL(technically referred to as the LM-2) concealed more than it revealed in its reporting format and not revised for 43 years. It is this maddening combination of indifference and impotency that allowed criminals to steal at-will in so many unions for so many years. The LM-2 finally had a revision in 2003.

Another agency, The Securities Exchange Commission, (SEC), works harder to protect shareholders, who by definition have money for campaign contributions and who vote. Union members have no such wealth and while they wield some collective political clout through their union PACs their individual contributions are dwarfed by the shareholder class both in terms of dollars and votes. There are over 94 million mutual fund shareholders in the United States and less than 15 million union members. (Some union members might be both but a distinct minority, I'm sure). 54% of Americans own stocks according to Gallup although 84% of stocks are owned by the upper 10% of wealth holders.

Many shareholders have no real power to influence corporate decisions that are made by the CEO or the board of directors. The Economist in February 2017 reports that "Do No Evil" Google set up a dual voting structure which insured that outside voters would have "little ability to influence its strategic decisions". Facebook came up with a similar structure and since has issued non-voting shares, a practice not unique to them. Snapchat's co-founders kept 89% of the voting power. Democracy be damned.

Senator Warren has introduced a bill, the Accountability Capitalism Act, that would give employees representations on boards, a great idea, after all who does the real work in corporations not the board or shareholders but the workers. The United States is an economic democracy on paper not in practice.

CHAPTER TWELVE:
I GET ANOTHER CHANCE

Ye shall know the truth, and the truth will make you mad
- Aldous Huxley

Then a break happened on the union front: I learned of hearings being held by a House Subcommittee, the topic "Union Democracy". I began contact with Peter Gunas and Lauren Fuller on the staff of the Subcommittee on Employer- Employee Relations chaired by Representative John Boehner (R-Ohio). I told them of my experience and urged them to hold a hearing on HEREIU. I kept contact with the subcommittee, by e-mail, for the next year. Despite being Republicans, but I was willing to deal with the devil to give my story on the International to Congress. But I had no intention to sell out.

In February 1999 I received a phone call from an associate producer of NBC's *Dateline*. He had heard about me from the Reader's Digest Eugene Methvin. He came right to the point, "Will you go on camera with your story?" I said, "Sure". I thought this was a tremendous opportunity by bringing the attention of the plight of the union to the public. Then create some pressure on the government to bring real reform to the union. After the "Dateline" call, the subcommittee staff called to inform me they would hold a hearing exploring union democracy in HEREIU, an event I did not view as a coincidence. I confirmed later they found out that Dateline would do a program on the union and I suspect that was the impetus to hold the Hearing.

During the following months I unloaded everything I leaned about the union on the *Dateline* producers. I sent them copies of the written material and documents I had kept and bombarded them with e-mail items as I recalled events and people. The information was invaluable to their research people. In June I was in D.C. for the on camera interview. I met the producers in the plush bar of the St. Regis Hotel. (Later, I saw the director frown at the bill.) Both likable and low key. We had a drink and talked about the union. The Dateline guys told me this was the "hardest job they had ever done since it was so difficult to get the people to talk". They shot some film of me the following day, shots of me at the Department of Labor Building and in front of the Capital (corny I thought). They even filmed me walking by the International headquarters. (I was hoping I wouldn't run into anybody and I didn't).

We drove out to Bethesda to a studio where I met the interviewer, a dark-haired woman with a patented smile and we began the interview. I never found my intellectual or emotional balance during the interview. I thought the questions posed by the woman were unprepared and somewhat inane. (In retrospect, I don't think we liked each other). I realized we had to inform the audience with basic info, but the questions seemed to be too casual and unrelated. What bothered me most was the lack of narrative flow as we jumped from one aspect of the union to another. I understood they would edit the interview into some coherent story but it was disconcerting to me not to have a logical linear flow (I think that way I guess). I was wired up, edgy and moved around in my seat before the filming. "Sit still" the producer said, he said in that deliberate voice a parent or a teacher would use to a child and we all laughed.

At one point we took a break. I saw the associate producer go over to the interviewer and whisper to her, "Don't forget to ask him about the Wisconsin local." I had talked about the Wisconsin local with the producers since it had been the reason for Hanley's resignation. I had to think hard about going public with the fact that I had provided that information to the government. The producers wanted this nice piece of drama for the program but I didn't want them using me just to make a good show. I delayed consent for a while and then decided to go public with it. I thought it was important to let other union members know their whistleblowing could bring results. When we resumed filming, the interviewer asked, and I acknowledged providing the information to the government about the Wisconsin local.

During the break, I told the interviewer as a casual comment that my mother had been a member of the union in Chicago. She later used this item to build a feminist aspect to the program by getting a picture of her from my brother. As much as I liked the idea of paying tribute to her I thought it was deviating from the narrative of the program. It just didn't seem to fit. I was uncomfortable with the interview. I didn't think the program was good. When the interview was finished. I turned and told the producer, "I don't want to watch this". He seemed comfortable with it telling me I did "Fine." It didn't feel "fine".

It also upset me with myself for blowing the point that members could file civil RICO suits against unions that might be defrauding them. I forgot it. I left the studio unhappy with the interview and also disappointed with the producers who seemed somewhat amateurish to me. They were new at it.

I had a busy time in D.C. I met with the Subcommittee staff that same week and provided them with information that would help during the hearing. I would keep contact with them until the hearing on July 21, 1999. As someone who voted Democratic 95% of the time I understood too well the anti-labor bias of Republican legislation. Therefore, I find it hard to believe to this day that the Republican party which fights so ferociously against even a minimum wage for working people and equally aggressively for business interests is truly for the average working person. However, the staff surprised me and seemed concerned with the lack of a democratic process in HEREIU and union corruption. Gunas was pleased with the meeting, "you've had a pretty productive week," "First Dateline and now us", he said. Gunas was a big man with a smooth practiced political manner but had a certain candor I liked.

They talked straight-forward with me. I told them, "I'll cooperate as long as the thrust of the effort is anti-corruption and not anti-union." They seemed to understand that. They told me I would have five minutes to testify. I mentioned that it would be hard to distill 12 years of experience with the issues in five minutes. They gave me an extra minute (such are the protocols of hearings). I worked hard on editing my statement for weeks but when I read it aloud the night before in my D.C. hotel room it startled me to realize it still ran nine minutes (reading aloud differs greatly from reading silently). I worked until after midnight editing the paper down (and every word I cut seemed like a physical amputation).

I experienced some fear as I walked from my hotel on Capital Hill to the Rayburn Building. The staff had offered me a hood to cover my face to testify anonymously, but I had brushed that aside as overly dramatic. When I got to the staff's office, the fear has disappeared. I was just on time. "I knew you'd show up" Gunas smiled as he shook my hand. It occurred to me that he may have been more relieved that I showed up as opposed to being sure that I would. I met two other witnesses, one from the San Francisco local who would talk of union democracy in that local and a young Latino from Chicago who was running for election in Local 1. We talked for a few minutes before the hearing.

The San Francisco guy was from the HERETICs the so-called dissident group of the union. He was a pudgy hard drinking waiter who had passed the law exam but never practiced law. He was an articulate guy but somewhat immature and ego-driven. I had corresponded with him before the Hearing. Only about ten people were active in the group. A reporter had characterized them as "gadflys" and that was an apt description. Well-intentioned, good at getting some publicity, but more rhetoric than action. They had no desire to form a viable dissident group but merely to complain. One of the group, Michael Rose formerly from the Las Vegas local, did the most constructive and ambitious thing by starting and maintaining, at his own expense, a website called the HERETICs where members could exchange views, anonymously if they preferred.

Only one, Ed Sinadaris, a fearless World War II veteran, took the challenge into his local in New York by attending and criticizing the leadership despite overt hostility. He told it as it is and despite the verbal abuse he suffered there was a begrudging respect for his guts. An active dissident group to reform the union never materialized in HEREIU partly because of suppression by the union, the large turnover, as well as apathy of the membership and a lack of leadership in the ranks.

They packed the hearing room with union people, many of them wearing yellow union tee shirts. I saw some familiar faces including the editor of the HEREIU newsletter, the propaganda organ of the union that provided literal and figurative cover for the union officers for years with ghost written articles by the editor presenting the officers in a glorified manner. There were a few International vice-presidents present and John Wilhelm, the new president of the union was there to testify as was Mullenberg the monitor, along with officials from the DOL and the Department of Justice. Both Dateline and the union filmed the proceedings. Later looking at a photograph of the hearing I saw later, I recognized Frank Massey standing in the room's rear. (For him, the "handwriting on the wall" was there if he chose to read it).

Physically, the hearing room seemed more mundane in reality than it appears on television; its ambiance had the sterile, functional quality of a school auditorium. Each of us had a microphone and a red light bulb on the long panel table in front of us. I was on the end seat next to the court reporter (who kept bothering me during the hearing asking me how to spell words. I should have told him to buy a dictionary) The subcommittee, flanked by staff, was facing us. Some panel members, somewhat disconcertingly popped in and out of the hearing, ostensibly to answer roll calls or vote (or perhaps go to the restroom or get some coffee).

Chairman Boehner made an introductory statement. Boehner had an unusual, almost eerie presence. His face and body had a clarity that was unreal. He reminded me of a hologram of a human being rather than a real one. (The chairman, who handed out tobacco PAC money on the floor of the House to representatives, is a smoker and had no compunction about the effect of secondhand smoke on his staff in their small office off the hearing room). Later Boehner mentioned, as an interesting personal aside, that his father, a bar owner was a member of the union for over 40 years. He is currently involved in the cannabis business on the advisory board of Acreage Holdings. (I hope he isn't smoking that stuff).

I spoke briefly with Boehner during a recess which allowed members of the panel to vote and the rest of us to take a break. "So what are you doing these days?" he was asking whether I was working. "Nothing much,", I said trying to avoid the smoke haze he was giving off, "Just some volunteer things". I was more interested in the hearing than my economic welfare. "Do you think anything positive will come out of these hearings?" Boehner was reading something on the desk. He took another drag and blew out more smoke: "Sometimes just shining some sunlight on a problem is a good thing" he said. I said nothing and just moved out of the smoke haze. I interpreted the answer as a cliched piece of BS that congressmen threw out to constituents when they couldn't or wouldn't do anything about an issue.

Some time later they indicted Frank Massey, and he pleaded guilty in July 2003 to fraudulent filings of a construction union's annual report to the DOL. Massey was lumping unclassified expense account items, which represented 1.5 million in an officer's personal expenses on the annual report as "Office and Administrative" or "Education and Publicity" expenses obscuring their real nature and purpose. He got a break on his sentencing for cooperating with the government and wound up with a $30,000 fine and $5000 restitution to the Labor Department There should have been strong fines imposed on the accounting firm for the membership because of their inexcusable negligence of the years which let Massey and others let the officers diminish the union's assets. I'm sure the Congressional sub-committee hearing led to DOL scrutiny of his audits. Boehner might have been right about shedding some sunlight on things helps.

The panel of representatives composed of Democrats and Republicans (in the majority), immediately fell into their partisan stances. The Democrats going on the attack with Representative Miller of California, a big, impressive man with a powerful voice, the designated hitter to attack the Republicans. He began by accusing the Republicans of attempting to undermine labor and of "union bashing". It was clear he was out to set the tone of the hearing by putting the Republicans on the defensive.

Miller, whose PAC contributions are loaded with union contributions, was more concerned with playing to his union audience and potential contributors than correcting union corruption. The Democratic attitude reflected their own compromised position, namely the huge campaign contributions of labor both in money and manpower, which precludes them from taking any meaningful action to correct the oversight flaws which allow union corruption to flourish for decades. Their concern for their campaign contributions far outweighed any concern for the union members.

The Republicans for their part acted remarkable genteel. I think a strategy was in place *not* to appear as union-bashers.

This strategy failed, however, in that the Democrats under Rep. Miller's lead seized the initiative in the hearing and didn't let it go. (Later Peter Gunas was asking, "How did we let Mr. Miller take over this hearing?") Most of my life I have avoided public speaking because of shyness. In high school, I would skip the classes where I was scheduled to speak. However, in this, the most important speaking engagement of my life, I wasn't nervous at all. I was wired with determination, all feelings shut off, and my mind focused. I was the first witness.

I led off with a strong indictment of the government's failure to implement democratic process in the union and for not attempting to recover the millions of misappropriated union funds. I talked of the many financial abuses, my attempts to change things by working with the government, my effort to get the DOL audit team to expose the abuses. Also, the failure of the accounting firm to do its job and the dominance of the union by Hanley. I brought up his Mafia mystique and his refusal to testify before the Senate committee. (Rep. Miller would later refer to my criticism of Hanley's silence before the Senate Hearing saying, somewhat sarcastically, that he didn't know that not testifying under the Fifth Amendment was an admission of guilt. (I was tempted to ask him if he suspected his wife was having an affair and asked her about it and if she pleaded the Fifth Amendment whether that would leave him comfortable with her candor).

I ended my testimony challenging the participants in the hearing to implement democratic processes, i.e., direct elections for general officers. I'm not sure exactly how long I talked but when I finished the red bulb warning light was blinking and I could see Chairman Boehner becoming uncomfortable. The witness's testimony, including mine, follows this writing and is also on the web. Federal Reserve Chairman Alan Greenspan testified before Congress the same day preempting me from appearing on C-SPAN. (I'll never forgive the Chairman for that; I respect C-SPAN and would have like to have had myself and the issue on it).

The subsequent testimony could not have improved my point. The monitor's comments appeared defensive and unconvincing. He made the unusual claim he was not aware of the immunity agreement between Hanley and the government, although he had signed off on his resignation. Responding to my claim about conflict of interest, he also claimed he had no voice in the selection of the review board. He did not recover the union funds but urged the union to do so, (in a classic buck passing maneuver President Wilhelm testified afterwards he wouldn't do so because the monitor didn't do so). Wilhelm did not address direct election of officers. Wilhelm wrote Mullenberg complaining of lack of fairness by having two critical witnesses (me and the Heretic John Palewicz) and no positive members. He invited Mullenberg to join him in Las Vegas for a study of HERE. In Vegas?

Wilhelm, a portly, dynamic and capable man, had accomplished some good organizing work for the union. Hanley selected Wilhelm to be his replacement when he resigned from the union. On July 31, 1998. (Wilhelm succeeded as president and elected president at the 2001 general convention.) Wilhelm, essentially honest, signed off on everything Hanley proposed during his years at the union and later turned into an apologist for him. Wilhelm, after noting some of Hanley's accomplishments, dramatically declared he would have resigned if they had found any of the national leadership to have organized crime connections. (He seems to overlook Hanley's taking the Fifth Amendment 54 times before the 1984 Senate Hearing or his acceptance of a ban to communicate with Local 54 because of Mob ties) hiring known hoodlums like Ralph Natale., John Lardino, Frank Gerace, et al.

The government clearly stated Hanley's relationship with the Mob in the above actions. Hanley's sister married into the Mob. Hanley was the brother -in-law of Frank Calabrese a notorious and ruthless Capa who led a Mob crew in Chicago and who was a prime figure in the famous "Family Secrets" trial in Chicago in 2007 which decimated the Outfit. 14 indictments which included 18 unsolved murders prosecuted.

Calabrese's son, Frank Jr. turned informer on the Outfit and wore a wire for the FBI. Later his Uncle Nicholas Calabrese flipped and became an informer, the combination of which resulted in a series of convictions on important Mob figures and long jail terms and sent Frank Jr.'s father to prison for the rest of his life which incidental ended in 2012. Omerta has given away to "No Honor Among Thieves". On YouTube Frank Jr. rejects the label of a rat and still lives in Chicago. In the old days, he would be long dead. The FBI site proudly carries a summary of the case which they say sent a "Who's Who of the Chicago Outfit to prison. They did a great job and people who I never thought would go to prison would spend the rest of their lives there.

Apparently Wilhelm did not know of Hanley's early presidency of Local 450, a local started by hoodlum Joey (doves) Aiuppa or the hiring known Mafia types by Hanley in the International during his administration. Didn't find his arrest for carrying a gun in Las Vegas unusual. Should I believe he didn't know about ex-convict Chicago's Barney Grogan, an errand boy for Hanley, who made no secret about his doing time in Alcatraz. Did he have any reservations about Hanley's failure to move against the rampant corruption in several proven Mob connected locals? It's a tough sell to believe that a smart, savvy guy like Wilhelm after many years in the union would not know what was common knowledge about Hanley's connection with organized crime figures.

Perhaps he meant he was waiting for unimpeachable evidence, but I think sometimes we like juries have to rely on circumstantial evidence and probability in making judgments. But then many people ignored it including the AFL-CIO, the Chicago Catholic Cardinals, and the Cook County Democratic Organization which held a $125 a plate dinner honoring him in May 1997. Denial seems to be expedient. The monitor stated he found "no evidence of Hanley having Mob connections" The government had a hard time proving Mob connections also but that doesn't mean they didn't exist.

Professor James Jacobs, who has followed and written extensively on organized crime influence in unions said, "Whether HEREIU has been purged of La Cosa Nostra influence is an open question". He was skeptical of Monitor Mullenberg's report calling it "The least intensive and comprehensive" of the monitor-ships of the four international unions calling it "Brief, scantily staffed and minimally intrusive." "We do not know whether HEREIU has been substantially liberated." I'm not sure about how clean the welfare funds were. I know at the time there was at least one Mob connected individual on the funds who I pointed out to Mullenberg but he left him there untouched.

Wilhelm was a member of the executive board for years overlooked and therefore collaborated in the financial rape Hanley conducted on the union by concurring with his signature on all the outrageous spending propositions. He later said it was a spending style of unions a style that almost bankrupt the union at one time and squandered the member's dues money. I saw no evidence of any protests by him over any of the irresponsible spending. The RICO action by the Justice Department named the General Executive Board as a defendant charging them with multiple illegal acts to defraud the membership. The monitor could have and should have removed all the executive board, including Wilhelm, for violating their fiduciary responsibilities to the members. Wilhelm did not try to democratize his union by calling for direct elections. His concept of democracy didn't include the members of his own union. Even the Teamsters and Laborers now have member elections.

Wilhelm and HEREIU went through an ugly split with Unite in 2009 after their merger in 2005. He and Bruce Raynor his Co-president and former head of Unite got into a power struggle. When the ferocious fight was over HERE came out a winner in the settlement which left them with a high-rise in Manhattan formerly owned by Unite and worth 136 million dollars. The union is headquartered in the building, renting out the rest. Wilhelm retired with laurels from the union in 2012.

Mr. Yud the spokesman for the DOL, a stereotype bureaucrat, humorless, rigid in his necktie and suit, read from a prepared script. He read through a litany of statistics: the number of unions the DOL audits, the number of elections they monitor, a full monologue which eluded any explanation of the financial tragedy which took place at HEREIU. Mr Yud, his eyes never leaving his script, defended his section's role in auditing the union saying that while the law establishes financial safeguards for unions and fiduciary responsibilities for officials these are enforceable only by union members through lawsuits and the DOL does not have that authority under the statute. They do, however, have authority to refer potential criminal cases to the Department of Justice. The DOL saw fit to do this only twice with the International despite the many violations detailed in the monitor's report. Both of the referred cases languished at the DOJ.

A post hearing statement from another DOL official who took great pains to plead with the subcommittee to keep any documents sent there confidential showed the catch-22 absurdity of the DOL's sorry oversight of unions and inadequate enforcement. It explained, at length, that all audit information and results considered confidential and not available to the membership or public, (as a matter-of-fact not even through the Freedom of Information Act). Yet they place the burden of bringing complaints on an uninformed membership.

A House Workforce and Education Subcommittee asked the National Labor Relations Board to look at the Havey audits of over 700 unions, citing them as "unreliable". Thomas Havey considered one of the top five accounting firms in the country with 700 union clients folded. The DOL revised the annual report to make it more meaningful and recommended civil penalties for the chronic late and non-filers. (This is the same DOL you may remember, who along with the Department of Justice, went on record as maintaining that there was no need for and they had no plans to make any changes relative to their procedures).

So we have the farcical scenario of one official maintaining the members are required to file lawsuits on perceived labor violations and the other official declaring that all audits are confidential. I experienced deep disgust when I heard the DOL and DOJ officials state that they say no need for any procedural change in their respective agencies despite the egregious failure to do their job at the International (and one could add the Teamsters, Laborers and many other unions to the list). Strictly standard bureaucratic bullshit.

I was assertive during the Hearing interrupting it three times to get the chairman's permission to speak. I challenged the DOL comments on putting the onus on the members to file lawsuits by again pointing out the fact that the DOL kept all audit information confidential not available to the membership. At another point I brought up Hanley's alleged organized crime connections telling the Hearing, "We ought not gloss over this issue" and repeated the failure of the monitor-ship to recover any of the diverted union funds. I criticized the government's tendency toward expediency rather than justice in dealing with union corruption.

Representative Andrews, a New Jersey Democrat, the ranking minority chairman, surprised me by saying, "Mr. Giblin. I appreciate the long years of attentiveness to this problem and I share your frustration, your testimony will be very valuable to us". I nodded my acknowledgment of his recognition. I appreciated his appreciation.

As the Hearing neared lunchtime, I realized it was almost over and I had a touch of panic, nothing was happening. I had worked long and hard for this day and now it was evaporating before my eyes and ears. Knowing I was being aggressive, I asked again to make a comment. Boehner said, "Yes but quickly," I reinforced a comment by Mullenberg of the need for the DOL to can file lawsuits to ensure the fiduciary responsibility of officers and then I said that "I fear that this will end without addressing what we are supposed to be addressing, and this is union democracy"

"We should ask Mr. Mullenberg why the ability for the union members to directly elect their officers wasn't implemented in this RICO action. We should ask him whether the Review Board has the power and will exercise the power to bring democracy to this union. But they have made much of 47 recommendations, what about a recommendation for direct elections for these union members? This doesn't take a prolonged legislative effort. This can be done very easily."

Chairman Boehner ended the Hearing immediately after my comment. The Hearing turned out as I had feared: a political catharsis, with compromised legislators locked into their political stances, more concerned with partisanship than the Mob corruption which held captive and exploited hundreds of thousands of American workers for decades. I wish I had called the subcommittee on it right then and there. I wish I had told them that the hearing was an exercise in political bullshit and left the hearing. I still fantasize myself doing that once in a while.

The whole experience was a hard lesson in civics. I had always kept some faith in the political process, despite years of reading reports of the ugly machinations of politicians and although I understood about union influence in politics I kept some faith. When the media alluded to the practical political motivation of politicians, I thought they might be rather cynical and overlooking the humanity politicians must have in them to some degree.

The Hearing was a wake-up call in political realism for me and confirmed my worst fears about the integrity of politics. The Republican staff members seemed delighted with my performance "You did good," Lauren Fuller said, smiling. I heard the same thing from people I didn't know. An FBI agent came over and shook my hand. "You're the only person who said anything here today," he said. I talked briefly with the Dateline producer. He admired my effort, but I noticed they interviewed the young man from Chicago and it surprised me they weren't interviewing me also for the upcoming program.

What I realized later was that they would not cover the political reasons for corruption in the union. They pursued entertainment value not investigative truth. After the hearing, I walked to a nearby restaurant with the Chicago and San Francisco union witnesses and had a beer and sandwich with them. We rehashed the Hearings a little. I had the sense that while we didn't expect much from the Hearings, we all felt better by having testified. I tried to encourage them to file RICO suits, "Sue the bastards," I said.

Talking with Peter Gunas right after the Hearing, I asked him if there was any possibility of legislation arising from it, "Not with these guys on the committee", (meaning the Democrats) he said. In a later conversation with him I thought he might have been sounding me out about joining the staff. "You get things done," he said at one point. That may have been my imagination but as interesting as it might have been to get into the political process I could not, would not work on a Republican staff.

Afterwards, I received a form letter signed by Boehner informing me that under Title 18 of the US Code, any retaliation for my testimony was illegal and prohibited by law, (like I'm supposed to carry the letter around with me and show it to anybody that has a contract on me). I knew that there was now another element of risk in my appearance and testimony. They saw what I looked like now, (with beard) and that I was in North Carolina. They must be getting fed up with me by now and I must have generated a lot of hostility by my words and actions. The removal of Hanley meant that the cash cow was dead, and it also meant that the hundreds of people who benefited from it would no longer be nourished from its milk.

They could even believe I was entirely responsible for the government intervention, (I wasn't; the government had that plan for some time). They didn't know what information I gave the government, but likely and correctly attributed things like the revelation of the Wisconsin local to me. I had pointed out several locals and people I thought deserved a hard look and that had resulted in the removal of some officers when the monitor conducted his investigations. I doubted they would act while the government was still involved but one could never be certain about those things.

I went back to Chicago. I looked at condos on the north side and in Evanston. Chicago still had a deep hold on my psyche but if moved back I would never be comfortable answering the doorbell and I decided not to go back. I would always have a concern, conscious or unconscious every time I walked into a restaurant or bar that I would run into someone who knew me, who hated me for what I had done, and would act on that hatred. That possibility was one I didn't want to live with. So I didn't.

Instead, I drove to D.C. where I spent the next two months trying to put together a civil RICO suit which might recover some millions stolen from the union over the years. I was very unfulfilled by the failure of the government or the union to recover any of the member's money diverted for personal use by the officers, it deeply offended my sense of justice. These guys blatantly loot the union for decades and their punishment is that they it allows them walk with their loot intact. I envisioned the suit as going against the former officers, the DOL, and the accounting firm for their respective responsibility in the financial fraud of the union.

I connected with Art Fox who agreed to help me find an attorney would do the suit. I had received assurance from the dissidents that they would join in the suit. I worked very hard day and night during those months researching the issues at university law libraries and supplying the attorney with facts that would support the case. I prepared a letter for local pro bono attorneys and waited for the attorney to help.

The help never happened. Fox, who has done a great deal for the labor movement, was busy filing a Supreme Court brief and then dealing with family affairs. I had the sense from the beginning he was operating more from obligation than motivation. I offered him an out, "Look", I said, "I know you've got a lot going with your family and job, send the stuff back to me and I'll take it from there". He sounded relieved, "Sounds good" he said. I got the material back that week. In the interim the dissidents support started to fade. I contacted some pro bono attorneys directly who expressed little interest in the case.

The suit never developed, a shame because it would have set an important precedent in holding officers financially responsible for their corrupt acts and putting the DOL and the accounting profession on notice that they had better do their jobs. This would have been an important tool for members to use to protect their interests. It also would have provided the ability to recoup assets that had been diverted for personal use and provided for treble damages (if you can't send them to jail, send them to the poorhouse). I have often believed that my "friends" in the reform effort have been almost as much a detriment to the cause as the Mafia types, at least one knew where they stood. The so-called reformers aren't there for you when you need them, a reality that is hardest of all to take.

CHAPTER THIRTEEN:
I LOSE MY FIFTEEN MINUTES OF FAME

There will come a time when you believe everything is finished,
that will be the beginning
- Louis L'Amour

In December I got a call from an associate producer of Dateline telling me they wanted to do some additional shots of me sitting at a computer and talking about some things I found in the union. I told them I'd do it but I wanted to talk about the RICO lawsuit I thought the membership should file. This point was one that the Dateline producers had been reluctant to mention until a lawsuit was filed and Sandler gave me no direct response on the demand. I had a premonition that something was going wrong with the program. The additional shoot meant they weren't satisfied with the original effort. Sandler said he would like to see more "passion" by me on the issues. I had decided the evening before to focus on the issues rather than dramatics, but that turned out to be the wrong approach.

It's always interesting at what gets lost in the process of production when more people get involved in its development. Sandler startled me when he said that some people wanted to know what I had contributed to the whistle on the union that the monitor hadn't ferreted out. He seemed to have forgotten my 16 page letter to the monitor which the monitor had acknowledged and followed in his investigative efforts and which included the critical Wisconsin revelation. My premonition was right, ten days later Sandler called me and told me the shoot was off and an event that had taken place in the union had bumped my program. The

International had trusteed Local 1 and Dateline would cover the reform candidate's efforts to get elected as officers in the local.

My cause was lost (and my fifteen minutes of fame) I denied any sense of disappointment over my not getting any recognition for my efforts and instead focused my regret on the issues not being publicized. Much later I realized it would be nice to know old and current friends and acquaintances saw me on the program and appreciated what I had done. I wanted recognition more than I admitted.

The program, "The State of the Union" aired afterwards in late December and depicted some financial abuses, the Mob connections, the monitor's efforts and the reform candidates in the Chicago local. While it was good entertainment and human interest, it covered none of the of the basic systemic failures that led to the corruption in the union, i.e., the DOL, the accounting firm, the politics. They leveled no criticism at the monitor; no mention of the need for a more democratic process in the union. The congressional hearings were not even mentioned. So much for the "Hard investigative reporting" MSNBC touts for Dateline.

I complained to the producers asking why they ignored the big issues. They acknowledged the systemic problems but said it was too much to do in one program, "It would take another whole program to cover those issues" an executive producer said, responding to my complaint. Recognizing entertainment is what TV is about, it still seems to me that investigative reporting should look at social issues along with entertainment if it is to be respected as such.

Four weeks after the Dateline show, Ed Hanley was killed in a head-on collision near his Wisconsin retreat on January 7, 2000. He was killed instantly and the other driver injured. He was on his way to pick up a pizza. I got a call from the Labor Notes reporter asking me if I thought it was a gang hit and I told him, a little sarcastically I admit, that I didn't believe the Mob was into suicide hits yet. No evidence that the crash was Mob-related has ever been found. I took no satisfaction at the news of his death although it was significant, since Hanley despite his removal, still had some potential residual influence over the union and now that was gone too.

He did not get to enjoy his three pensions, lifetime salary, personal expense account, automobile, etc. There was some nice irony in that but I would have preferred to see Hanley receive justice in a courtroom and to take some of those perks and personal assets from him while he was alive. He died with a salary of $270,00 a year. He had the foresight to arrange that in 1973 after taking over the union by ushering a proposition through his rubber-stamp executive board that "because of the strains of his job that may "overburden any man's physical endurance" he could retire whenever he chose and receive a full salary for life. And then he was just 42 years old. (He should have had that pizza delivered.)

To allow people to spend a career looting union dues and walk away from it is not a deterrent to future union criminals. A lawsuit that would recover union funds diverted for personal use would signal to both the criminal and the victim it was a crime that could be rectified. A successful suit would have empowered and emboldened the members to seek justice when they found corruption in their union. When prison time wasn't available as a punishment, going into the personal pockets of the perpetrators would could be a nice punitive and painful alternative punishment.

Disgorgement, recovering stolen monies from personal assets has been used in RICO suits and most drug enforcement wherein the government seized even the homes of known drug dealers that had profited from illegal acts. This kind of financial justice is appropriate for both union officers and CEOs who abuse their trust. I also believe that a punitive amount be added to the recovery to compensate the victims for their betrayal. That would be real justice. It still bothers me that the reform and justice that should have taken place has not happened and that this whole scenario will be played out again. Wilhelm and HEREIU has cleaned out some remnants of the Hanley days but there is always the possibility of the Mob moving back in when it senses the time is right.

In Chicago, the Outfit has suffered some hard times in the past decade with leader after leader going to prison. Their overall activities curtailed although they still kept some operations going. Like corporations, they downsized and become more efficient. Mob hits are rare; The Mob has become more business-like, black listing rather than blow torching. In fact, what they've done is made investments in all kinds of legitimate business operations. They are dormant but not dead.

The past two decades saw a rise in the status of whistleblowers making them more acceptable. There has been a sharp increase in the number of people blowing their whistles. Time magazine nominated three of them as "Women of the Year". I've some reservations about one selection. It is true Sharon Watkins, the Enron executive, blew an internal whistle to her boss Kenneth Lay first in a letter dated August 15, 2001, in which she voiced her concern over the special purpose entities' accounting techniques and their potential impact on *Enron as a corporation and her future*.

Her effort was covert in that the letter was anonymous. In doing so Ms Watkins seemed to be acting out of "enlightened self-interest" rather than public interest since she failed to notify employees shareholders and the public of the problem. There have been many whistleblowers who acted out of real altruism and deserve the status of heroes. But somehow I don't see this individual, despite her public acclaim, deserves that title and acclaim she received. Forbes magazine in a 2002 article made the same criticisms with the headline, "Sharon Watkins Had Whistle But Blew It"

And Jeffrey Wigand's motivation seems somewhat mixed. Again he raised questions about tobacco safety to his superiors and after they rejected his concerns he stayed around for two years collecting a $300,000 a year salary. After being fired in 1993, he signed a confidentiality agreement. It was not until the company broke that agreement that he took it to the public. This doesn't seem to me to be a motivation driven primarily by public interest, like Watkins he won acclaim as a hero after "60 Minutes" and a movie. Far from destroying Wigand, whistleblowing made him.

The False Claims Act (FCA) of 1963 gives up to 25% of recovered funds which involve fraud on the government to whistleblowers. Referred to as Qui Tam, (Latin abbreviation meaning He who sues on behalf of the King and for Himself) 7002 whistleblowers triggered recovered funds of 2.9 billion dollars in 2016. 53.1 billion has been recovered since 1986. In a few rare cases rewards amounted to over a hundred million dollars to one person. Bradly Birkenfeld got a record $104 million for blowing the whistle on UBS (also got 40 months in prison for his part in it). I find these rewards excessive, but I have no objection to whistleblowers being well compensated for the risk, the pain and punishment they endure.

The average whistleblower reward under FCA is 1 million dollars (not bad) However, the time to process a suit can be years. The DOJ declines 80% of the whistleblower FCA cases brought to it. (The Chamber of Commerce in its usual business biased manner, tried to undermine the FCA in 2016 but the Supreme Court voted 8-0 against it), a rare victory for the good guys. A number of states have initialed their own FCA laws. Some employers started reward programs for whistleblowers in their organization. This is good but can be problematic with employees looking over their shoulder and petty dislikes, resulting in bogus whistleblowing. But you can't have it both ways and I consider those rewards represent a progressive program.

I never expected financial reward and gotten none On the contrary I sat down one day and figured out what I lost and projected losing in salary and retirements benefits over the years will amount to almost a million dollars. It may sound like a pretentious cliche, but the reward of having done the right thing has been priceless and no amount of compensation could equal that reward. In fact, any kind of reward would dilute the meaning of the mission.

I never coveted luxury, in fact it always made me uncomfortable; what I've always wanted was freedom, to be free enough to do what I wanted to do and not to do things I didn't want to do. That's what money has always meant to me. Assuming my mutual funds don't go south too far and I don't incur any extraordinary medical expenses I'll get by. And I can always do some accounting work. And most importantly, I've got that freedom.

So no regrets about the financial sacrifices, at least, so far. I have some regrets over the enormous time, my life, that I devoted to this cause and I would like to get some of it back. Time becomes more precious as one ages and I acutely understand how fast it goes. In retrospect, I would work smarter not harder.

My one man effort was worthy of Don Quixote, or at the end of the day, as they like to say. I have no single conclusion on my experience: although a well-intentioned mission, it was unrealistic; Despite the long, hard, risk-taking search for the so-called silver-bullet, ironically, I found that the item that led to the removal of the president easily. A secretary winked and mentioned to me that a new local had opened up in Rhinelander, Wisconsin. I knew this was a recreation playground for Chicago people and that triggered my decision to look at it more closely. Remarkably, despite its Quixotic nature, the mission was surprisingly effective in removing Hanley, changing the course of the union and triggering some systemic reforms although more are needed.

So it was a mixed bag of results which seems to be the stuff of "life". The reality is that I don't take much credit internally for what I accomplished. It is not so much what I achieved, but that I did what I had to do and it's no big deal. I experience mixed feelings about even writing about the experience. I am proud that I had the conviction, (both of which I had always doubted in myself), to do what I did and the impact I had on the union and the union movement. The experience wasn't transforming, which may have been an underlying hope and fantasy. I have the same fears, anxieties, problems as I always had, but it gives my life a kind of meaning that it would otherwise lack and because of that I am glad I did it. I would blow my whistle again without hesitation. I made that difference I wanted to make.

I am in North Carolina living on my early retirement pension of $571 a month (with no cost-of-living clause), social security, and my savings. I had hopes of making some money doing grant writing for non-profits, a task I found useful and rewarding. As it has turned out to date, I've volunteered a lot more than earning money but that's okay too. Not to tell a tale of penury I am living off money earned from the investment of the small fortune I had saved while on the road with the union. This takes care of my basic needs and then some. I am not middle class maybe lower middle class or something like that. Whatever. I own, (about one third of my mortgage principal), a modest ranch in with a state park as my backyard: wonderful woods, deer and a variety of wildlife and a river 75 yards away. I can swim in it in summer. I've trained my neighbors to respect my need for peace and quiet after years of living in noisy apartments. I found my refuge. I relish it.

As I write this and relive the experience, I realize that at no other time in my life did I feel such purpose and meaning. I miss it and almost wish I were back there again hunting, exploring, going through files in the middle of the night, collecting information, dealing with the bad guys, trying to change things. However, there are few fears of retaliation anymore. That threat is passe, (which may be why I write this story for publication now, but then again this might trigger some old bad feelings so I will keep my shotgun). The threat may be more legal than physical now.

Unions used libel lawsuits to suppress honest criticism of officers in the past, however, there are free legal resources now that will help me if I should run into that problem. And I've said some things that might offend some but Truth is the first line of defense in a libel lawsuit and if this story is nothing else, it is as true as I could humanly make it. And counter-suits are always possible. I don't think too many people will want to challenge these facts and suffer the publicity the truth would bring on them. We'll see what happens.

I like to believe my motivation was to correct the injustices I saw the union inflict on its members and I believe from my dedicated efforts at one level that is true. However, at another deeper level I may also have been trying to correct the injustices done to me as a child. Hanley, the Irish hard drinking, wild spending union leader, was like the profligate father I had and the exploitative neglect of the members was like my family's neglect. I had suffered the same pains of poverty that they suffered so my outrage was for both of us. In a real sense I did it for myself and for the members. And an important corollary motivation was that I consider it very important to bring the issue of whistleblowing and its value to society to the public. I believe my experience and others shows that value.

Analyzing one's motivation, getting past the neat self-serving answers, isn't always pleasant and can lead to endless introspection, but one can't escape the why of their behavior either. I ask myself if I would become a whistleblower if I hadn't been rejected as a child and developed a kind of detachment and distance from life? Would I have been a whistleblower if I hadn't experienced poverty and had a passion to fight it? Would I have been a whistleblower without the ethical influence of Humanism? I think the honest answer is that it is likely that I would not have been a whistleblower without those influences, but there were other more subtle motivations involved.

Some say it is impossible to write an objective memoir from a subjective point of view. Probably true. But I've tried hard to keep this honest going back and revising things I thought might need clarification and adding some others like my turbulent teen years. I believe the good/kind things I've done significantly outnumber the bad things I've done. I included little about my rather boring sex life or my secret fantasies but I'm okay with that because this is a personal memoir with a social theme not a confessional memoir although I've acknowledged some failings. There's a difference. I will say I've been intimate with about six women but not experienced a "great" love affair, perhaps few of us do. There are no great sexual exploits or lurid experiences to tell you. While I freed myself from the great guilt, the Catholic Church puts on one about sex, i.e.,lust, lasciviousness, carnality, etc. I'm not sure I ever got beyond a residue of that emotional influence.

C. Fred Alford, a professor at the University of Maryland who likes to mix political theory with psychoanalysis, (a mix more potent than anything a bartender could conjure up), wrote a book, *Whistleblowers: Broken Lives And Organizational power*. Alford spent much time with whistleblowers in small support-like groups listening and thinking about their experiences. On his opening page, he discounts a theme raised in other books that most whistleblowers, despite their suffering, would do it again if they had it to do over. His findings were that they wouldn't do it again *if they had a choice)*.

He quotes one man who lost his job, his house, and his family and his lawsuit. The man a professional engineer wound up delivering pizza and owed $50,000 in legal fees. The man's words are both telling and poignant: "So, I think I was crazy to blow the whistle. Only, I don't think I ever had a choice. It was speak up or stroke out. So all I can say is that I wouldn't do it again if I didn't have to. But maybe I'd have to. I don't know". Honest, decent guy.

Professor Alford found that two-thirds of his subjects lost their jobs, a number which coincides with other studies. A number lost families and slid into depression and/or alcoholism. As one might expect from someone steeped in psychoanalytic theory, the professor goes in depth analyzing the motives of whistleblowers. Going beyond right or wrong and altruism, he focuses on that old psychoanalytic concept of *narcissism*. He calls it *moral narcissism.* In Alford's view the whistleblower almost has to act to avoid being corrupted by the organization he/she sees to be corrupt. Their ego ideal, their idealized self-image is threatened and therefore they cannot do otherwise then blow the whistle. He doesn't see the moral narcissism as a derogatory label, in fact, he respects it.

Interestingly, the alternative to quitting the organization is not considered a viable alternative by the whistleblowers in these studies (although I considered it). They either seem to believe that their revelations will lead to change once people understand more about it and/or that quitting would be cowardly leaving the bad situation unchanged. I think both motivations are at play in their decisions and in mine.

So professor Alford attributes whistleblowing to the need to maintain an ego ideal the whistleblower has an idealistic vision of him or herself and has to blow the whistle to live up to that ideal. I believe this need also played an important role in my whistleblowing. I had to do it to live up to that ideal. *Not* doing it was not an alternative, it would have lessened an already shaky self-esteem. So my personal psychological reasons along with social justice concerns provided the powerful motivation for my whistleblowing.

When whistleblowing is discussed today, the names of Snowden and Manning often come up. A person's moral conscience is superior to any oath to government assuming the results are overwhelming on the positive side. The moral duty is to oneself and to the public not the government, corporation or even to an individual. Candice Delmas of the Department of Philosophy and Religion says there is "something like the public's right to know" and guidelines for leniency when prosecuting whistleblowers should be provided. She further states in her paper on *The Ethics of Government Whistleblowing"* that protections given to conscientious objectors could provide a legal basis for protection to these whistleblowers". A very thoughtful paper.

When I encourage whistleblowing, I am not advocating a society wherein everyone is turning everyone else in for something or blowing the whistle on friends for interpersonal injustices. In a human sense we all cut people a little ethical slack. What I am talking about are serious wrongs and what I am saying is that there are injustices that cry out for correction and that, if we as a society embraced and enforced the idea of whistleblowing as an expected and accepted norm. We could make a fundamental change in our culture for the better.

Check out https://www.spj.org/whistleblower/whistleblowers.asp how whistleblowing has changed society. We could achieve much of this transformation on a personal level by our own actions and just do it, not waiting for legislation which, when it comes, is in a very belated, after the fact manner with enough holes in the law or enforcement features to render it mediocre in effort and result. With enough whistles being blown, corporate and union miscreants would ponder hard before they started or continued bad acts. Like motorists on the expressway, these people follow the speed limit laws when they are being watched and might suffer consequences. The trick is to keep watching and keep blowing the whistle when they exceed the ethical speed limit. Here is a link to Wikipedia that has a comprehensive and fascinating list of whistleblowers from 1777 on: https://en.wikipedia.org/wiki/List_of_whistleblowers

I have no foolproof advice for potential whistleblowers, one has to follow their own needs, circumstances, and conscience but it is critical to realize the realities before acting and to realize that even though the whistleblower is doing the right thing, society rarely cares about the right thing but more often the expedient thing. A whistleblower may in publicized cases, reap some recognition and reward and some whistleblowers land on their feet finding new careers and opportunities. But in more situations they reap only punishment, isolation and regret. The only real reward comes from within, the knowledge that one did the right thing no matter what the consequences. It comes down to something intrinsic in a person, something profoundly personal, a belief in what's good, what's right, what's just and the deep need, both personal and societal, to do something about it, to blow the whistle.

Hugh Giblin

APPENDIX

(7 pages of testimony and a picture of myself and witnesses being sworn in at hearing).

Committee on Education and the Workforce
Subcommittee on Employer-Employee Relations

Hearing on
"Union Democracy, part VII: Government Supervision of the Hotel Employees & Restaurant Employees International Union"
Wednesday, July 21, 1999

<u>Opening Statement of Chairman Boehner</u>

Witness List
Committee on Education and the Workforce
Subcommittee on Employer-Employee Relations Hearing on
"Union Democracy, part VII: Government Supervision of the Hotel Employees & Restaurant Employees International Union"
Wednesday, July 21, 1999
<u>Opening Statement of Chairman Boehner</u>

Witness List

Witnesses are sworn in by the Chairman

<u>Hugh Giblin</u>
Former HEREIU Accountant
Chicago, Illinois
<u>Pablo Garcia</u> (**PDF**)
Local Union 1 Shop Steward
HEREIU
Chicago Illinois

<u>The Honorable Kurt W.</u>
<u>Muellenberg</u>
Former Court-Appointed Monitor
& Member of the public Review
Board HEREIU
Washington, DC

Maria Elena Durazo
Local Union 11, president
Los Angeles, California

Jonathan Palewicz
Shop Steward
Local Union 2/HERE to Insure
Change
(HERETIC)
San Francisco, California

John W. Wilhelm
General president
HEREIU
Washington, DC

John C. Keeney
Assistant Attorney General,
Criminal Division
U.S. Department of Justice

Lary F. Yud, Chief
Division of Enforcement
Office of Labor Management
Standard
U.S. Department of Labor

http://commdocs.house.gov/committees/edu/hedcew6-63.000/hedcew6-63.htm

Mr. Hugh Giblin
Statement
Before the
Subcommittee on Employer-Employee Relations
Committee on Education and the Workforce
July 21,1999

I am very pleased that the sub-committee is holding this hearing and showing its concern for the matter of union democracy in general and in particular the lack of democratic process in HEREIU.

As someone who was administrative aide for six years in the union at the International level I have had a unique viewpoint of its activities. As an accountant I took a special interest in its financial life. As a union member I took strong interest in its treatment of its members. I was appalled at what I discovered in both areas. So appalled that I contacted federal law enforcement agencies offering my help in ending corrupt practices.

I will not go through the long litany of financial abuses that existed and are detailed in the fourth report of the monitor who investigated the union as a result of the Civil RICO suit by the DOJ in 1995. I have never in 35 years of accounting experience in a wide variety of settings seen such reckless and wanton spending, lack of generally accepted accounting standards and indifference to essential management procedures. Furthermore, there was a pattern of systematic financial exploitation of the membership to enrich themselves and their friends. There was only superficial respect for democratic process and the well-being of the membership.

Millions of dollars were channeled into: 10% annual officer's raises, lifetime salaries plus pensions for officers, excessive and undocumented expenses a huge fleet of 60 leased autos which the monitored determined "were assigned to individuals who use them primarily for commuting and personal use rather then union business". per diem abuses, a bloated payroll which at one point absorbed nearly half of all union revenues and far exceeded comparative international union expenditures and was permeated with friends and relatives, a number of whom had no qualifications and no work accountability. There were consultants whose "retainers" totaled hundred of thousands of dollars a year who filed no reports, the abuses go on and on. There were and are credit cards for retired officers, and ongoing per diem payments, leased automobiles, pensions, and lifetime salaries.

The monitor-ship found very serious quantitative abuses over the very limited life span of his engagement; if one were to go back and perform an audit of over two and a half decades of financial abuses the amount determined would be staggering. There seemed to be no limit to the creative greed of these individuals and no inner moral sense to restrain them. To support their lucrative lifestyles they consistently raised the per capita tax, that portion of membership dues, paid to the international union until it was one of the highest in North America. And these dues come from one of the most financially marginal occupational groups in organized labor and our society.

The abuses ran unchecked and unabated for 25 years. One could ask how such a situation could continue despite periodic audits by the audit staff of the Department of Labor and annual audits plus an ongoing presence of the certified accounting firm. The abuses were transparent, some directly violated the Landrum-Griffin Act and criminal in nature. The DOL and the accounting firm would noted the lack of accounting standards but their efforts were feeble and futile and the follow-through inadequate and ineffective; the problems continued year after year and it was these very lack of basic accountability which allowed the financial rape of this union for a generation. These accounting "deficiencies" were designed to obscure and prevent accurate accounting for union funds so that financial diversion of union funds could continue. This effectively gave greedy union officials a perpetual blank check to buy whatever they wanted, when they wanted it because they knew there would be no audit trail of accountability.

Let me give a precise example: the annual report of the labor union to the DOL makes this statement, "it is not practical to make a precise distribution of automobiles expenses." This is an accounting cliche used with rare validity in this day of computers. I saw this term also used relative to the accountability of credit card expenses. What it really means is that these expenses are not being accounted for as generally accepted accounting standards require and in this case what it means is that expense records being deliberately obfuscated.

The DOL has a statutory obligation to protect the membership of unions from these abuses by audits which under Title 29, Sec. 431(b) requires financial information "IN SUCH DETAIL AS MAY BE NECESSARY TO ACCURATELY DISCLOSE ITS FINANCIAL CONDITION." "IN SUCH DETAIL" is the mandate not what is "practicable". I believe an examination of the DOL audit reports over the past 25 years would prove my contention that they were aware of these abuses, repeatedly failed to correct them, and in doing so allowed this outrageous exploitation of the membership to continue. I confronted the DOL after their 1991-2 audit and in person at offices asked why they didn't act on these abuses. Their response was "we don't like it but its up to the membership to do something about it". These audits are not released to the public let only the membership. How, if they could considering MAFIA intimidation, would they be aware of these financial failures to do something about them?

The accounting firm has a fiduciary obligation to be independent and report the financial condition of its subject audits objectively and fairly to third parties including our membership. As a former auditor I find it incomprehensible as to how these accounting irregularities and financial abuses could continue for decades by the accounting firm charged with reporting on this union's financial condition. There are accounting standards, audit procedures and ethics subscribed to and maintained by the profession. I am asking the AICPA the American Institute of Certified public Accountants review this firms relationship with HEREIU over the years to determine if they acted professionally and ethically. A professional, ethical audit is the only protection dependent third parties have whether they be members of a union or shareholders in a corporation.

These organizations failed the membership in these respective obligations and allowed financial misfeasance to continue unchecked. I believe the committee should ask "why and how" this outrage could exist for such a long period and I feel better audit and disclosure procedures should be implemented to avoid such further financial tragedies. One piece of the solution might be to give the current members audit committee some real substance (rather then the ridiculous 2-day ritual it presently is). Also provide it with the ability to be an ongoing rank and file committee which has privy to all financial events effecting union funds. These committee members should be selected by the membership at large rather then the Secretary-Treasurer and should have the ability to publish their findings in the union newsletter. Whose money is it anyway?

I used the word tragedy earlier and tragedy is not too melodramatic word to use. The abuses at the international coupled with the serious mismanagement and fraud in the welfare funds, an experience which was not mentioned in the civil RICO and covered in the monitor-ship. This resulted in two DOL lawsuits and the loss of many millions of dollars in benefits is a tragedy. I have an aunt, ladies and gentlemen, who retired after many years as a housekeeper and member of this union on $45 a month and this was in the 1980s not the 1950s. What existed at HEREIU was a literal dictatorship placed into office by bought, intimidated or helpless delegates. Further there existed an uninformed membership who had no direct electoral vote of the general officers who used their authority to gain complete control of the union and its finances.

Dominating a completely compliant executive board they got whatever they wanted whenever they wanted it. I will give you two telling examples of my charge. I examined 500 proposals for expenditures presented to the general executive board; the monitor in his investigation examined 837. In total there were six negative votes, and 22 abstentions. The abstentions were usually related to salary increases for the person abstaining. Six "no" votes out of 1337 proposals. No record of debate or further explanation of the expenditure. A rubber-stamp executive board.

What president Hanley wanted: Sabre jet, motor home, condominium, jobs for unqualified friends and fees for consultants who never filed reports, etc. president Hanley got.

The second example relate to the present electoral process. The members elect delegates from their locals to the general convention. These are often officers or business agents. Unfortunately the delegates and their locals are often beholden to the president for favors, support and other help. This process has shown itself to foster one-party systems in unions which lend themselves to abuses of power. In HEREIU this process coupled with the intimidation resulting from the president's organized crime connections created the dictatorship and financial havoc I alluded to at the start of this statement.

I authored a white paper prior to the 1996 convention detailing many of the abuses later documented in the monitor's report. I mailed a copy to all of the delegates. I gave sources for every charge in the paper. No one. Not one person, raised their voice as president Hanley was voted in by acclamation without discussion or debate on Monday morning of the convention week. This I suggest is not a democratic process or representation of the membership.

When the news of the Civil RICO reached me I was delighted. I had been waiting for it for years. I wrote a ten-page letter outlining my concerns and observations to the monitor; I stressed in letters to the DOL and the DOJ the need for direct elections. However at its termination I was disappointed and dismayed. The DOJ in its initial suit had stressed the need for "a return of democracy to this captive union." The conclusion of the monitor-ship did not provide for those two basic necessities of any democratic process: an informed electorate and the right to vote. Judge Brown who oversaw the action and Mr. Mullenberg, the monitor neglected to put into place direct elections of general officers, a process incidentally which was seen to be necessary and implemented in the Teamsters and laborers RICO actions.

This is irresponsible and inexcusable. It violates the spirit of the consent decree and the spirit of democracy our nation claims to exemplify. How can the leaders of our nation point critically to the lack of democracy and human rights in other nations if here, right in our backyard cannot implement democratic processes for hundreds of thousands of workers and their families? This egregious failure also undermines the intent of the consent decree to preclude future abuses through organized crime influence. The members have been denied the only tool they have to remove corrupt general officers - the vote. They also ignored the other vital ingredient.

While the initial RICO action was published in the union newsletter, none of the proceedings of the monitor-ship were published. This is in complete contrast to the Teamster's monitor-ship where every event was published monthly especially as they related to organized crime. The monitor-ship did, under pressure put in a final one page commentary at the end of the monitor-ship. It would seem to me that since it was the memberships dues that paid the over three million dollars cost of the monitor-ship that the members had the right to know in detail the financial abuses perpetuated against them. Who the perpetrators, and in fact all the details of the monitor-ship not a perfunctory one-page summary. Knowing organized crime figures were being removed from office would have been a crucial encouragement to the rise of democratic elements in the union membership.

It would also seem to me to be appropriate, while we are to review the review board a little. The board set up by the consent decree comprised of an ex-governor who has received funding from the union and whose wife did legal work for it and a clergyman whose seminary and church have received very heavy contributions from Mr. Hanley whose charitable largesse to personal causes with union funds was questioned in the monitor's report. It is intriguing and instructive to note that the "ethical canons" developed by the review board forbid even the "appearance of any conflict of interest" by union officials but apparently this particular ethic does not apply to the review board itself. All the rhetoric flowing from the DOJ and monitor-ship on union democracy would have more resonance if they appointed a rank and file member to the review board. Whose union is it anyway?

The participants in this hearing has a rare opportunity to accomplish change in this union with no prolonged legislative effort. The public review board has the power, spelled out in the union constitution to end the lifetime salaries of the officers. This is an absurd gift to men who have lived opulent lifestyles off the hard work of one the poorest segments of our working population. They have more then adequate pensions. Mr. Hanley has 3 pensions and a 401-k, a 650,000 estate. I don't think we need worry about his future security but we should be concerned about the membership's security. The perks for retired officers that I alluded to earlier should be abolished.

The review board should recover from Mr. Hanley and any other participants the hundreds of thousands of dollars of union funds spent to create and maintain for five years the bogus local in Rhineland, Wisconsin. It was used as a cover for writing off expenses so he and others could play in their vacation homes. Why shouldn't the monies from this documented fraud, a criminal offense under LMRDA not be returned to the union treasury? Mr. Hanley resigned rather then face charges for this specific financial malfeasance. Why hasn't an effort been made to recover the hundreds of thousands of dollars paid by Tom Hanley while president of Chicago's Local One to his father for "advice" This arrangement the monitor found "breached his fiduciary duty" and resulted in Hanley Jr.'s suspension. The principle of disgorgement has been established in civil RICO law by law enforcement. The monitor-ship recovered 28 thousand dollars from Mr. Hanley and Mr. Leavitt for manipulating auto leases. This is a token gesture and an insult to the membership and the meaning of justice.

Is it justice to remove officials after long careers of financial misfeasance and malfeasance? Are we to believe forced retirement of men into the privileges I have described represents a determent to future corruption by others? I don't think so. I do not believe that the membership should not bear the full burden of the RICO cost, an event that was not created by them but by the corrupt officials of their union. These officials should bear a significant portion of the cost of this RICO action. Again there is case law under RICO which has seen this very just fine enacted. The review board has the power to do this and give the members at least this much justice. They will never get back the millions converted and wasted by these officials in the past 25 years.

This monitor-ship, like a surgeon treating a seriously ill patient, surgically removed a number of officials. Well and good, the patient looks and feels better. However this is treating the symptoms not the disease. There is no meaningful preventive medicine here. It is unlikely all the disease has been removed; there will be new agents of the same disease and it will metastasize again as soon as the patient is on their feet and medical supervision is removed. This has been a palliative RICO and the patient/union will be seriously ill again.

Again an example: I was told by the monitor after the report that the duration of the review board was uncertain and that they would meet four times a year. He was unsure of his own time commitment. If this is the totality of supervision, it is inadequate and appears to be the government's effort to find a gracious way to exit the union but leaving it again vulnerable to all the evils it has endured an I say this with absolute certainty, it will endure again unless we do something about it here, today. Solutions such as creating an in-house database that tracks criminals border on silly. Beyond the expense and expertise needed to accomplish this it would seem to me law enforcement is already doing this and could provide this information to a union if requested. And since when do all criminals have criminal records?

I recommend the review board, the DOL and the accounting firm look at what changes can be made in their oversight to strengthen future financial audits and give complete disclosure to the membership. This will allow them the ability to exercise their judgment as to the quality of their leadership and protect their rights by their own civil RICO suits if necessary. The review board has the power to implement direct elections in this union. It is beyond belief to me to have a declared mandate to bring democracy to a union without implementing direct elections. If we asked the high school students how to bring democracy to this union, I'm sure the "right to vote" would be echoed again and again. Yet somehow this most singularly obvious and essential mechanism to initiate democracy and prevent the gross abuses of power in the past in this union escaped our seasoned government officials.

HEREIU has many dedicated able union people who have suffered under the abuses of the Hanley administration and who given the proper democratic framework could become one of the best unions in the country. The participants in this Hearing have the power give this union some much neglected justice by ending the financial abuses that continue and recovering some member's dues. They can give this union the same democratic process in the workplace of their livelihood that we enjoy as citizens in our country, that is to vote our convictions and protect our rights.

I would urge the sub-committee to consider and recommend the actions I have suggested and that the appropriate people implement them as soon as possible.

Hugh Giblin

ABOUT THE AUTHOR

I am from Chicago, now living down south. I've been writing for years, I had a 5000 word feature article published in a national magazine, poetry published in local literary journals and online magazines and two plays produced locally. As an accountant I worked in corporations, CPA firms, the IRS for a year, and ultimately the non-profit sector. I blew the whistle because I grew up in hard poverty and identified with the union membership. I also had a strong sense of right and wrong, a dislike of injustice and a belief in justice.

NOTE FROM THE AUTHOR

Word-of-mouth is crucial for any author to succeed. If you enjoyed *The Whistleblower's Tune*, please leave a review online—anywhere you are able. Even if it's just a sentence or two. It would make all the difference and would be very much appreciated.

Thanks!
Hugh

Thank you so much for reading one of our **True Crime** novels.
If you enjoyed the experience, please check out our recommendation
for your next great read!

The Poisoned Glass by Kimberly Tilley

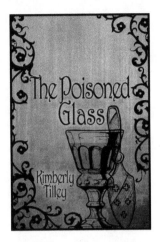

"A great read and a fascinating retelling of a long-forgotten murder,
that still resonates to this very day...
for anybody interested in the history of the Silk City!"
–Mark S. Auerbach, City Historian, Passaic, New Jersey

CPSIA information can be obtained
at www.ICGtesting.com
Printed in the USA
FSHW011734220520
70359FS